*"You don't really need a reason
to spend time on a river, do you?"*

—ROBERT CARPENTER

Exploring America's
Wild & Scenic Rivers

By Douglas H. Chadwick

▢ NATIONAL GEOGRAPHIC
WASHINGTON, D. C.

For every river that causes the adrenaline to surge,
there is another that bestows deep tranquility.
PRECEDING PAGES: Bearing waters, sediments,
nutrients, and fry from as far as the upper slopes of
the Canadian Rockies and Wyoming's Teton
Range, the Columbia rolls through its
final obstacle, the coastal Cascade Range.

Rivers Lost and Rivers Won

MERCED RIVER *Arising in Yosemite National Park, the Merced carries clear water, trout,*

and reflections of the Sierras—the Range of Light—down toward California's Central Valley.

"Any outdoor pursuit which brings a man into intimate contact with natural scenery, natural forces, and the unaltered web of life is highly educational. The right to experience this should be as inalienable as freedom of worship."

—JOHN CRAIGHEAD

ALL WINTER LONG, the Rocky Mountains stand silent in a freezing sky while passing clouds cover them with water in the form of wafer-thin stars. Then, each spring, that white mantle shifts from its crystalline state to a restless one. It goes traveling. Drop by drop, liquid beads from the snowpack, pulses, trickles, shimmers, pools, and spills over to join other rivulets, sluicing faster and faster and gathering strength until suddenly, one warm day, every crease in the slopes holds a cascade and the cliffs are striped with waterfalls, and their silver thunder echoes across the high country. If, as they say, rivers have voices, this is their cry of birth.

Not all of North America's major rivers begin along the Continental Divide. But a good many do, like the Yukon's tributaries and the Noatak in Alaska; Canada's Fraser and the sources of the Mackenzie; the Snake and Columbia, which drain the U.S. Pacific Northwest; and the Rio Grande and Colorado, issuing from the Rockies' southern end. Although the continent's largest waterway, the Mississippi, starts its 2,348-mile journey in the lake region of Minnesota,

SMITH RIVER

California's last undammed major river system, the Smith and its tributaries, still supports runs of steelhead salmon (opposite) amid rainy redwood forests. Healthy rivers are also vital to songbirds, which find abundant food, shelter, and nesting habitat in riparian, or streamside, vegetation. In turn, the birds, like this waxwing by Wisconsin's St. Croix (above), help sustain the riparian zone by spreading seeds in their droppings.

its main tributary, the Missouri, forms from streams tumbling off the Rockies in Wyoming, Montana, and the Canadian province of Alberta and runs an almost equally long course of 2,315 miles.

A little east of Fort Benton, Montana, I let my canoe drift like a wayward log along a bank of the upper Missouri, the better to watch a bobcat drink. I've hiked and floated some of the clear headwaters, but this is already a different order of river, holding paddlefish and buffalofish instead of cutthroat trout and growing wider, smoother, and muddier by the mile. Having left the mountains behind to begin making its way across the Great Plains, the Missouri has become a great artery. I'm riding its pulse toward the continent's heart.

Boundless grassy vistas unfurl from the shoreline in places. Then the river will turn and furrow into that prairie landscape, exposing a foundation of old sea-bottom sediments and volcanic ash, and the view suddenly narrows to steep, striped stone beneath a ribbon of sky. Some of the walls have eroded into hoodoo terrain—a badlands array of pillars and fins along with stone mushrooms and strata honeycombed with caverns.

The river and its canyon sides, often referred to as the Missouri Breaks, amount to a ribbon of colors and contours that seems all the more striking amid the austere sweep of the high plains. Wildlife abounds, adding to the effect. While antelope roam the old buffalo hills, mule deer and elk graze the steep sagebrush gullies, and white-tailed deer appear down on the floodplain among cottonwood trees festooned with red-tailed hawks, magpies, and flycatchers. Canada geese guard nests on the willow-strewn islands. Great blue herons wade in the river among nearly 50 kinds of fish. There are even white pelicans summering here, as if to remind wayfarers that this current, this flow of high-country meltwater thickened with prairie grit, is ultimately bound for the sea.

"Rivers must have been the guides which conducted the footsteps of the first travellers," wrote the 19th-century American nature philosopher Henry David Thoreau. "They are the constant lure, when they flow by our doors, to distant enterprise and adventure....They are the natural highways of all nations, not only levelling the ground, and removing obstacles from the path of the traveller, quenching his thirst, and bearing him on their bosoms, but conducting him through the most interesting scenery, the most populous portions of the globe, and where the animal and vegetable kingdoms attain their greatest perfection."

It was the Missouri that, together with the Columbia, gave the travelers Meriwether Lewis and William Clark passage to the Pacific and back through the Louisiana Purchase, just obtained from France for three cents an acre. Consisting of most of the territory west of the Mississippi, it turned out to be a pretty good buy. The Corps of Discovery's 1804-1806 expedition gave Americans the first glimpse of just how far their new boundaries stretched and infused a young republic with frontier dreams.

To imagine the Lewis and Clark party moving along these channels isn't hard. My days, like theirs, are taken up by reading the eddies, watching the river-edge flights of the red-headed birds named Lewis's woodpecker, probing side canyons, and deciphering tracks. I can sense the kind of promise those men must have felt beckoning them onward. Now and then in the twilight, it is as though they were beside me, perhaps camped just out of sight a little farther down the sandbar under the emerging canopy of stars.

Hiking to the canyon's rim one morning, I am startled to find myself at the edge of a wheat field. I had almost forgotten my own era. One reason so much of the river corridor looks more or less the way it always has is that north-central Montana is still very lightly populated. Another reason is that the particular stretch I am paddling enjoys a special designation intended to preserve the natural and historic qualities that I have been experiencing.

I N 1976, 149 MILES of the Missouri in Montana were declared a wild and scenic river, thereby joining a national system of waterways protected under the Wild and Scenic Rivers Act of 1968. Like America's federal parks, wildlife refuges, and wilderness areas, the National Wild and Scenic Rivers system was the first of its kind in the world and continues to serve as a model for other nations.

Portions of 12 rivers were designated under the original act: Idaho's Middle Fork of the Salmon; the Middle Fork of the Clearwater and two tributaries, the Selway and Lochsa, also in Idaho; Oregon's Rogue; California's Middle Fork of the Feather; the upper Rio Grande

WILD AND SCENIC RIVERS

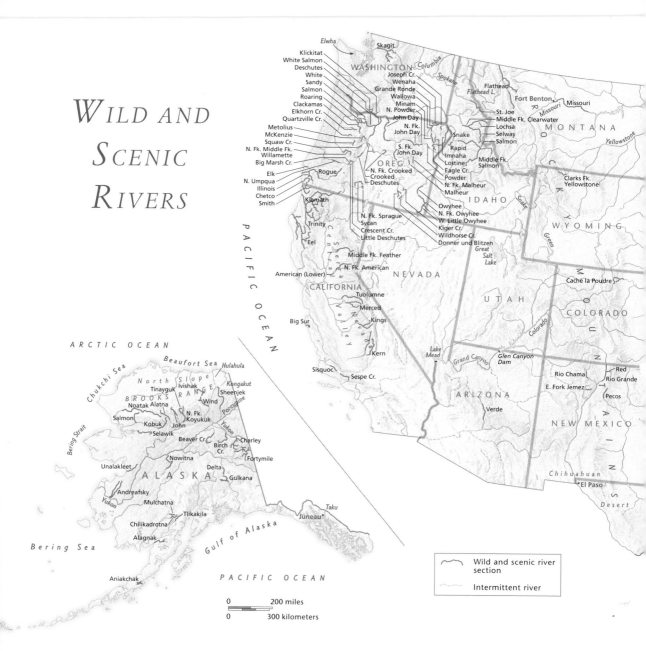

and its tributary, the Red, both in New Mexico; Wisconsin's Wolf; the St. Croix and its major tributary, the Namekagon, in Wisconsin and Minnesota; and Missouri's Eleven Point River.

Together, the protected lengths added up to 850 miles. The majority were in the West, which held the largest tracts of public lands along with the most rugged and intact backcountry. Another 27 rivers were singled out for study in the same legislation. A decade later, in 1978, the Wild and Scenic River (WSR) system had expanded to 43 rivers with a total of 2,299 protected miles representing a broader

range of geographic regions. Today, the system helps safeguard more than 11,000 miles along parts of some 160 rivers (more than 200, counting tributaries), from glacial whitewater rapids to black-water bayous full of alligator eyes. This array now includes another 98 miles of the Missouri where its course marks the border of Nebraska and South Dakota and the tallgrass prairie begins.

According to the Wild and Scenic Rivers Act (WSRA), sections of rivers within the system may be classified as either wild, scenic, or recreational. The terms have nothing to do with *(Continued on page 20)*

ANIAKCHAK RIVER Emerging from a volcanic caldera on the Alaska Peninsula, the wild

and scenic Aniakchak takes on the appearance of a fresh lava flow under the late evening sun.

ANIAKCHAK
RIVER

Where you find Alaskan salmon, like this sockeye being examined by federal biologists (upper right), you generally find grizzly bears. Well-fed on fresh fillets, cubs find plenty of time and energy to romp (above). The fish carcasses that they and older bears leave nourish a host of scavengers from bald eagles and ravens to red foxes (lower right) and wolves.

Aniakchak River Free to practice its artisanship on a grand scale,

the Aniakchak sculpts a volcanic landscape that is, geologically, almost brand new.

(Continued from page 13) the wildness, or turbulence, of the water or the difficulty of navigating it. They refer to the degree to which humans have influenced the river and its immediate environment.

Wild segments are "vestiges of primitive America" generally remote and in pristine condition, a watercourse version of wilderness. The scenic category is for portions that are more accessible but retain fairly intact shorelines. By contrast, "recreational" designates a segment that is handy to reach, relatively developed, and generally more crowded. Lonely or busy, pure or polluted, the one quality all have in common is that they are free-flowing. As a rule, only lengths of waterways without impoundments qualify for inclusion, although some, especially those in the recreational group, may have been dammed or diverted at one time.

*T*HIS CHAPTER is about how and why such a system came into being and about the directions it has taken since Congress passed the WSRA. The next three chapters offer excursions down three different rivers. Each highlights one category: wild, scenic, or recreational. First comes the Noatak, cold and far from human influences, flowing from Alaska's Brooks Range through Gates of the Arctic National Park and Preserve. Next is the Rio Grande, less wild in the sense that you can drive to a few points along the two protected sections but no less scenic. The upper WSR segment rushes down gorges of volcanic rock near Taos, New Mexico. Separated by more than 500 miles, the lower segment winds through even deeper limestone canyons that define the boundary between Mexico and Texas.

The example of a recreational river chosen for Chapter Four actually consists of three connected Massachusetts rivers: the Sudbury, Assabet, and Concord. Poised on the urban end of the WSR spectrum, in many ways they are about as tamed as waterways can get. Yet at the same time, they reveal the system's potential for reclaiming both the ecological health and the recreational pleasures of rivers in highly altered settings. The book's final chapter looks at current WSR candidates, the future of the system, and America's evolving relationship with the waters that run through all our lives.

Only a few generations after Lewis and Clark returned down the Missouri to St. Louis, the farthest reaches of the frontier had been claimed and the resources they contained were being rapidly consumed. By the middle of the 20th century, the nation had run short of the untamed places and creatures that were such a defining part of its heritage.

Nothing raises a commodity's value quite like scarcity. The rarer wild things became, the more precious people perceived them to be. Besides, Americans had more leisure now, and an increasingly citified populace wanted to enjoy it by getting away to the outdoors. No longer was conservation propelled in fits and starts by specialized groups such as hunters or birdwatchers. It grew into a broad social movement, especially as clean air and water—the most basic gifts of the environment, long taken for granted as a birthright—got harder to come by as well.

People were used to treating rivers as natural disposal units for sewage and garbage. Once the industrial revolution kicked into gear, adding a welter of novel chemicals to the waste mix, whole drainages began to sicken and die. Meanwhile, waterways everywhere were being dammed for hydropower to feed the country's explosion of commerce. More impoundments and diversions were put in for flood control, water storage, and shipping canals. The blockades raised water temperatures, altered or eliminated seasonal overflows, and made survival increasingly problematic for native plants and animals dependent upon the natural dynamics of rivers and their floodplains.

Two federal organizations, the Bureau of Reclamation and the Army Corps of Engineers, worked full-time damming and channelizing rivers to produce a variety of economic benefits. Many people's lives improved as a result. However, critics felt that as those bureaucracies expanded, they overstepped their original mandate and went on river-reconfiguring binges abetted by politicians eager to funnel construction dollars into their districts and industries seeking more federally subsidized power or irrigation. Not to mention speculators hawking waterfront real estate on newly created reservoir shorelines.

Whatever the case, the nation's rivers were eventually bottled up by more than 70,000 major dams and tens of thousands of smaller ones. The Columbia alone has 14 across its main stem, more than 250 across its tributaries, and chains of lakes lapping artificial shorelines for hundreds of miles where powerful currents once rolled. It was the greatest geologic change Northwest

ROGUE RIVER

One of the original dozen waterways designated under the 1968 National Wild and Scenic Rivers Act, Oregon's lower Rogue (below) became so popular that, within a decade, federal agencies had to limit the number of floaters to 12,000 per year. A decade after that, in 1988, Congress added a section of the upper Rogue (opposite), which comes out of Crater Lake through old lava tubes.

watersheds had undergone since the ice age glaciers receded.

Growing up in the state of Washington, I watched the dry bunch-grass country east of the Cascade Range blossom with new crop fields, orchards, and vineyards as irrigation from the corked-up Columbia sprinkled the equivalent of several more inches of annual rainfall onto rich volcanic soils. One tributary, the Spokane, runs through my old hometown, half-hidden in a canyon of warehouses and office buildings. As a boy, I used to make my way into the city center to bridges from which I could watch the water crash over Spokane Falls and jet from the spillway of the dam just above them.

It never occurred to me until much later that I was looking at the kind of place where salmon, glistening purple and silver, used to thrash, squirm, rocket, and high-jump up through the torrents in defiance of gravity. They were sockeye, coho, and chinook, and some of the chinook, also called king salmon, weighed 80 pounds, about as much as a kid on a bridge trying to figure out how the world works.

When Lewis and Clark navigated the Columbia, some 16 million salmon migrated in from the Pacific each year, traveling as far as 1,100 miles to spawn in various headwaters. Figuring the average fish to be, say, 20 pounds, 320,000 tons of sea-fed biomass came surging upstream, freely, almost miraculously, delivered within easy reach of eagles, bears, Indians, and then whites. Since frontier days, more than 90 percent of those wild salmon have disappeared.

Roaming the Columbia near its mouth now, I pass small towns where many a window is shuttered and fishing boats lie rusting in dry dock under drizzling clouds. Not only can I no longer conjure up images of the days of Lewis and Clark, I can scarcely envision the salmon fishery that was still a several-billion-dollar industry until late in the 20th century and, together with the fish themselves, shaped the character of the Northwest.

When I was nine years old, my father took me on a trip to Alaska. We boated part of the Kobuk River, which runs westward above the Arctic Circle to empty into the Chukchi Sea near Kotzebue. I was given a fishing rod and cast a lure into the current. It snagged after a while on a submerged log. Or so we thought, until I reeled in a type of giant white-fish known as an inconnu, or sheefish. Many years later the upper stretch of the Kobuk became an official wild and scenic river, but I will always think of it as the first waterway I knew that held fish the size of a boy.

Much of what wasn't dammed in the U.S. ended up ditched, dredged, and diked, straightened out to match the blueprint designs on engineers' desks. Other rivers were pumped virtually dry for irrigation. In modern form, the mighty Colorado barely seeps across the Mexican border into the Gulf of California, just as the Rio Grande often delivers no more than a trickle into the Gulf of Mexico.

Who hasn't driven a highway hugging one edge of a river while looking across at a railroad line hemming in the other bank? Being natural paths through the landscape, rivers attract parallel man-made versions. As new roads were pushed toward backcountry resources, more rivers found themselves confined by transportation routes.

Additional shorelines and the wildlife communities they support gave way to new industrial facilities and homesites. In rural areas, trampling and overgrazing by livestock reduced the natural vegetation cover, especially in the riparian, or streamside, zone. This led to more rapid seasonal runoff, increased erosion, and lowering of water tables. The problem was particularly acute in parched regions of the West, where river corridors serve as linear oases crucial to the survival of native species.

Geographers calculate that the U.S. contains about two million streams and rivers with a length of at least one mile, of which 10,000 run for at least 25 miles. The total comes to 3.6 million river miles nationwide. Outside Alaska, the great majority has been altered by development or degraded by pollution. Still, if only a small percentage remains in prime condition, it adds up to many times the amount currently within the WSR system. Across this vast, well-watered nation, there was, and still is, a lot left to preserve.

ONE OF THE FIRST notable efforts to save a wild river was by the naturalist John Muir, the leading early proponent of Yosemite National Park and defender of California's High Sierras. At the start of the 1900s he began a one-man crusade to prevent bottling up the Tuolumne River with a dam in Hetch-Hetchy Valley. The upper and lower reaches of the Tuolumne were protected from further dam proposals when declared a WSR in 1984. I keep the headwaters company for miles and days during a backpacking trip

FEATHER RIVER

Stones that stopped rolling gathered moss, encouraged by the extra humidity along the Middle Fork of California's Feather River, another of the original 12 flows protected under the 1968 act.

through Tuolumne Meadows and the bright granite highlands of Yosemite. Farther downstream, the river offers some of the best white-water boating in California. Yet between the two stretches, the Tuolumne goes flat and listless behind O'Shaughnessy Dam, and the Hetch-Hetchy Valley, once considered a scenic rival of the Yosemite Valley, lies drowned under the reservoir. You see, Muir did not win that turn-of-the-century battle.

For decades after his defeat, the pattern repeated itself. People might oppose a hydro project because it threatened natural resources or traditional recreation, or, in many cases, their own homes, farms, and villages, which stood to be inundated by the waters rising behind a dam. The plan would go forward regardless, and the battlefront would shift to the next river slated for harnessing. Every once in a while a development scheme was halted. But it seldom vanished for good. It was more likely just put on hold.

Born in 1916, John and Frank Craighead were building canoes and kayaks at an early age to explore wild, wet places. That they shared a passion for natural history equally wasn't surprising; they are identical twins. During the early 1950s the brothers were studying Canada geese on the upper Snake River, which begins high in Wyoming. They decided to have a look downstream in western Idaho at Hells Canyon, where the Snake runs through a gorge with walls rising nearly 8,000 feet up to snowy mountain peaks. One of the few parties to take on the canyon's furious white waters in those days, John and Frank emerged soaked, battered, and exhilarated. The experience prompted them to head for the even more remote rapids of the Salmon and its Middle Fork, formerly known as the River of No Return.

During the Korean War, the Craigheads ran training courses for military personnel in river and backcountry survival. Then in 1959, as if there weren't enough adventure packed into their days, they added a heap of grizzlies. Working in the Yellowstone region for 13 years, John and Frank carried out the first detailed study of these massive carnivores' biology, with support from the National Geographic Society. They pioneered the use of radio collars for tracking wildlife and, later on, techniques for tracking animals and analyzing habitats via satellite.

All the while, the twins kept probing the backcountry rivers of

MERCED RIVER *Let us pause by the water a moment to simply give*

thanks, for it is pure, flowing magic and the essence of life on this blue planet.

the West. The more they learned about those waterways and propos- als to dam them, the deeper their concern became. They began campaigning to ensure that some would always remain vital and free. "It is essential to preserve intact a few of the 'wild' rivers of this region for recreation and education of future generations," John was writing in 1957. "Any outdoor pursuit which brings a man into intimate con- tact with natural scenery, natural forces, and the unaltered web of life is highly educational. The right to experience this should be as inalienable as freedom of worship."

By 1968 three controversial dams stood across the upper portion of Hells Canyon. More impoundments were slated for the rest. Opposition kept them at bay until 1988, when the lower Hells Canyon joined the WSR system and became legally dam-proof. Which is why it still supports 10- and 11-foot-long white sturgeon, the largest freshwater fish on the continent. But in 1954, when the Craigheads started lobbying for waterways, there was no such thing as a national system to protect wilderness areas (the Wilderness Act would not pass until 1964) or endangered species (the Endangered Species Act became law in 1973), much less the last, best, and bright- est of the nation's free-running stretches of water.

Nor could Americans really grasp what was at stake. No nation- wide inventory of rivers and their qualities had ever been made other than from the standpoint of hydropower potential. The brothers out- lined a rating system to help set priorities by sorting rivers into four groups: wild, semi-wild, semi-harnessed, and harnessed, the first three terms being precursors of the wild, scenic, and recreational categories.

Wilderness advocates, fishermen in groups such as the Izaak Walton League, paddling clubs, author Sigurd Olsen (known for his descrip- tions of North Woods canoeing and natural history), and others added their voices to the movement. So did the National Park Service, with its longstanding commitment to wild resources. A statement in 1960 from the agency to the Senate Select Committee on Natural Water Resources reads, "...particularly in areas of dense population and in arid regions, clear natural running water is now a rarity and under the pressure of anticipated future requirements may become nonexistent. However, there still remain in various sections of the country natural free-flowing streams whose integrity might be preserved in the face of the water-control onslaught if conscientious planning to this end were applied."

The Senate Committee recommended as much in 1961. Next, in a 1962 report to the President and Congress, the Outdoor Recreation Resources Review Commission concluded that "certain rivers should be preserved in their free-flowing condition and natural setting" and that "recreation should be recognized as a beneficial use of water." These hardly seem like startling concepts today. But America had built a great economic engine dedicated to unlimited growth, and the frontier notion that nature stood in the way of progress was proving hard to shake. We were still on the rim of an era in which people touted plans to dam the Grand Canyon and Ohio's Cuyahoga River caught fire every now and then, fueled by all the petroleum leaking into it from Akron and Cleveland.

"Wild land has no pay-off time," John Craighead argued in one speech. "The use will be compounded by generations of Americans, and the totals will appear in the distant future." He went on to say that decision makers should weigh competing uses not solely for the present but for a time 50 years ahead, if not farther. Well, about 50 years have passed since he wrote that, and I doubt that even the twins could have guessed quite how enormous the demand for float trips, whitewater adventures, and other river recreation would be today.

*A*NOTHER BIOLOGIST, Paul Dowling, associated with the Nature Conservancy, had proposed setting aside "national rivers" in the 1950s. In 1964 Ozark National Scenic Riverways became the first. Five more were declared in later years. They include the Buffalo in Arkansas, a popular boating destination, and West Virginia's New River Gorge, which turns out to be anything but new; the current has been wearing its way into the bedrock since the Appalachian Mountains arose 600 million years ago. In essence, national rivers are waterways with a long, thin park enclosing them like a sheath.

The U.S. also has some 20 national recreation areas. Many of these are focused around waterways too, albeit fairly busy ones in some cases. For example, the Cuyahoga River, core of the Cuyahoga Valley National Recreation Area set aside *(Continued on page 38)*

SNAKE RIVER   From the right perspective, Hells Canyon of the Snake River looks more

like a slice of heaven, at least along this wild and scenic section by the Idaho-Oregon border.

SALMON RIVER

John Craighead (left) and his twin brother, Frank, developed an early passion for exploring untamed rivers and Idaho's Salmon (below) in particular. As wildlife biologists and lifelong outdoorsmen, they understood the importance of undisturbed drainages to native animals—and to the human spirit. When they saw how rapidly such waterways were being transformed by development, the Craigheads began speaking out to protect at least a sample of our free-flowing heritage. Their efforts were instrumental in bringing about passage of the 1968 National Wild and Scenic Rivers Act.

NIOBRARA RIVER *One of few national wild and scenic rivers in the Great Plains, the Niobrara runs by Nebraska's*

Fort Niobrara National Wildlife Refuge, which offers visions of the days when bison defined America's prairie horizons.

(Continued from page 31) in 1974, had been cleaned up since its flame-throwing heyday but still came with barge traffic and plenty of suspect chemistry. The 9,240-acre Chattahoochee River National Recreation Area in northern Georgia serves as a playground for the burgeoning city of Atlanta. For a while, the Great Chattahoochee Raft Race held the world title in the Guinness Book of Records for the sporting event with the largest number of participants.

The same year that the first national river came into being, 1964, a bill entitled the Wild Rivers Act reached Congress. In mulling over that and subsequent proposals, legislators accepted the wild part but pushed to include scenic and recreational rivers as well, hoping to make the conservation effort acceptable to a broader constituency. They succeeded. While not everyone is up to taking on an icy river going gangbusters down faraway mountain slopes, it gets hard to find somebody who wouldn't like to spend a little more time drifting along a weekend waterway savoring the sunshine and a picnic lunch.

*W*HEN THE NATIONAL WILD AND SCENIC RIVERS ACT finally passed in 1968, it did so by an overwhelming majority, and President Lyndon Johnson, who had supported the act, signed it on October 2. Legal jargon notwithstanding, the words of the bill have a kind of resonance. They should, for they are intended to echo beyond the lifetimes of those who formulated them: "It is hereby declared to be the policy of the United States that certain selected rivers of the Nation which, with their immediate environments, possess outstandingly remarkable scenic, recreational, geologic, fish and wildlife, historic, cultural, and other similar values, shall be preserved in free-flowing condition....for the benefit of present and future generations. The Congress declares that the established policy of dams and other construction....needs to be complemented by a policy that would preserve other selected rivers...."

Although early advocates envisioned wild and scenic rivers as a means of protecting whole landscapes, the act defines the WSR corridor as extending approximately a quarter mile back from each shore (a half mile in Alaska). The federal government is not empowered to zone or otherwise regulate the use of private property within that corridor. However, it can buy land from willing sellers. It can also arrange conservation easements, whereby a landholder agrees to forego certain types of development in return for a payment or substantial tax break. When all else fails, the government may acquire a property or right-of-way through condemnation. In practice this is seldom done, and the WSRA prohibits condemnation anyway if more than half the total acreage of a river corridor is in private hands.

The act also makes it clear that the federal government has no authority to acquire state lands along a WSR. Nor can it override a state's management of hunting, fishing, or water rights. So WSR status hardly amounts to a federal lockup of a river, as skeptics warned. The main thrust of the act is spelled out in Section 7, which says that the Federal Energy Regulatory Commission "...shall not license the construction of any dam, water conduit, reservoir...," or similar structure on any portion of a WSR. Moreover, no federal agency can approve a water resources project within the general vicinity if it would have a direct and adverse effect on the values for which a WSR was established. In short, the main thing federal control over a WSR prevents is federal harm to that waterway.

The system comes without a new bureaucracy to oversee it. Instead, management of each WSR is generally assigned to the federal resource agency with the most land within the river corridor or nearby: the National Park Service, U.S. Forest Service, Bureau of Land Management, or U.S. Fish and Wildlife Service, which handles national wildlife refuges. Where little or no public domain is involved, the Park Service, with its long history of preserving natural values, tends to be chosen. The agency also has a Rivers and Trails Conservation Assistance program for working with citizen groups to revitalize riverways, protect open spaces, build local trail and greenway networks, and link communities with their natural settings.

Occasionally, responsibility for some or all of a WSR is assumed instead by a state, by local governing bodies, or by Indian tribal authorities, such as where the Wolf River flows through the Menominee reservation in Wisconsin. About 30 states have systems of specially designated waterways apart from the WSR complex. These offer varying levels of protection along a total of about 13,000 river

MISSOURI RIVER Two sections of the 2,315-mile-long Missouri are set aside as wild and scenic: 149 miles in Montana,

shown here outlined by autumn cottonwoods, and another 98 miles downstream, bordering Nebraska and South Dakota.

miles. Section 11 of the act directs federal resource agencies to help the states safeguard rivers through their own systems or alternatives.

No country had ever crafted a conservation measure like the WSRA before. Where some laud its strengths, others find weaknesses; the quarter-mile shoreline corridor is such a narrow strip, they say, that development on state and private lands can still degrade a fully protected WSR. Just the same, this was the best the republic could come up with in 1968. The act wasn't meant to be a finished product. It was intended as a starting point.

Besides authorizing the study of 27 more rivers, the WSRA called for the kind of nationwide river inventory that the Craigheads and others had been suggesting for years. The different public land agencies were supposed to evaluate the potential of each waterway running through lands under their jurisdiction. Their eagerness to do so has a way of changing with different administrations. A recent effort identified 3,400 free-flowing river segments with one or more of those "outstandingly remarkable" natural or cultural values mentioned in the act.

All rivers are magnets for life. After all, most organisms consist mainly of water, whether they are aquatic or land based. This is why, across a major portion of the continent, the highest biological diversity—the richest array of plants and animals—is associated with wetlands and streams. It follows riparian corridors through the landscape. And since the boundary between two ecosystems will hold wildlife typical of each area plus creatures adapted to the juncture itself—a phenomenon known as the edge effect—biodiversity can be greater yet where the riparian corridor contacts neighboring habitats.

For humans, all this translates into a concentration of fish, game, and edible plants. Add fertile soils, ready access to drinking water, and a means of transportation and trade, and it becomes obvious why cultures throughout history have gravitated toward flowing water. I would be amazed to come upon a river that did not have, as the WSRA puts it, "....remarkable scenic, recreational, geologic, fish and wildlife, historic, cultural, or other similar values." Are they outstandingly remarkable? How do you define that? Every politician and interest group may have a different answer.

A proposal for a WSR must pass through Congress twice; once

for authorization of a study and the second time for approval based upon the findings. The other main route into the system is for a state to decide that a river deserves WSR status and have the governor ask the secretary of the interior to grant it. Even after joining the system, a new WSR may have to wait for federal, state, and local authorities to come up with a mutually satisfactory management plan. Some rivers still lack one a decade after being declared protected.

THE FIRST RIVER that Congress added to the dozen named in the original act was the Chattooga, found where North Carolina, South Carolina, and Georgia meet at the southern end of the Blue Ridge. It was designated in 1974, and the principal purpose was to stop a series of proposed hydroelectric dams. This river does throw off an aura of power, no doubt about it. From its origins atop the Appalachian escarpment, it falls more than 3,000 feet in 57 miles before reaching Lake Tugaloo, which backs up behind a Georgia-South Carolina dam. Of the WSR miles, 40 are in the wild category, tumbling through parts of three national forests, including Ellicott Rock Wilderness.

River runners grade rapids on a scale from Class I, which beginners can handle, through Class VI, which should be taken to mean, "this water can eat your boat and puree your body, and a portage around it is a really good idea." Much of the Chattooga is a series of white-water shoals, rock gardens, ledges, sluices, backwash hydraulics, and falls rated Class III (medium difficulty) to V (the maximum most experts will risk). Since the early 1970s, 35 people have died running this river, which won wide renown as the setting for the 1972 hit movie *Deliverance.* WSR management has cut the risk by giving boaters and rafters better information, requiring them to follow safety guidelines, and closely regulating commercial outfitters. But with the number of annual visitors having soared to around 90,000, the Chattooga still drowns somebody almost every year.

"Not on our trips," Phil Baxter, a high school English teacher who has guided on rafts for 18 years with a company called Southeastern Expeditions, tells me as I hop aboard and grab a paddle. "Two other companies have commercial permits, and they've never had a customer drown either. *Um...,* there have been a couple

ST. CROIX RIVER

As these cross-country skiers prove, you don't need something that floats in order to travel the St. Croix. You just have to wait until winter turns it to crystal. Counting its tributary, the Namekagon, this is the longest wild and scenic river in the eastern half of the nation, with more than 250 protected miles in Minnesota and Wisconsin.

of cases of heart attacks in the rapids." He isn't kidding.

The upper Chattooga offers sections that canoeists with modest skills could handle. But we're headed into the river's lower reach, the roughest part, where Seven Foot Falls promptly throws young Tyler Cooney from the raft as it roller-coasters toward a wall of rock. His father, Gary, hauls him back aboard in the pool below and tells me that this was easier than when he jumped in to retrieve his daughter on an earlier Chattooga trip. Then Deliverance Rock and Raven's Chute appear. In between following Baxter's urgent paddling commands, I glance up to see two—no, make that three—people tumble out of the raft in front of us and start to drop down a diagonal sluice. Soon, all that remains visible are their helmeted heads bobbing along through the froth like ducks that landed in the wrong spot.

We are a party of four 12-foot-long rafts loaded mostly with young teens from a school in central Florida. By the time we break for lunch, six of them have been overboard at least once, as has one of the fathers. Even the drier ones among us are chilly despite the raft company's wet suits and life jackets, for it is a rainy, early spring day with fresh snow in the highlands nearby. My impression is that a third of these people are having the time of their lives. Another third look pretty sure that they are being led to their doom—the black vultures soaring over the gorge aren't doing much to dissuade them—and the rest don't know what to think.

I think the Chattooga qualifies as outstandingly, remarkably extreme. It kicks butt—literally. Knocking a few folks overboard is just par for its course through the lower gorge. That's why the guide team includes what I call catchers—skilled kayakers who go through the rapids first and linger below to haul any swimmers to safety—and positions people with throw ropes at the worst spots. Those are coming right up, by the way: First Falls, Corkscrew, Crack in the Rock, Jawbone, and Sock-em-Dog, another seven-foot drop. Everybody okay? Here we go.

All you can do is paddle hard and hope the helmsman's aim is true and maybe talk to yourself or your god a little as you enter a chute and feel flumes of water grab the raft and shoot it forward as if someone had just switched on booster jets. Baxter positions us almost perfectly. As we fly off Sock-em-Dog to splash-land in pessimistically named

St. Croix River

In early America, the Namekagon and St. Croix were an important route of passage between the Great Lakes and the Mississippi. Today, people from the nearby twin cities of Minneapolis and St. Paul flock to the rivers for recreational travel. Some exchange paddle power for dog power after freeze up. Husky and malamute sled dogs, like this team en route to the main riverway, happen to be especially close to the ancestor of domestic dogs—the wolf, making a comeback in the same Great Lakes region.

Dead Man's Pool, marking the end of the cascades, I'm wearing a big ole grin. It is the expression of someone who considers the price of this float trip a real bargain for a combination heart checkup and adrenal gland flush with prayer practice thrown in. On the bus trip back from our pickup point, I see more smiles and hints of newfound pride on the younger faces around me as well.

*T*HE WSR SYSTEM expanded slowly at first. But the early hopes of the Craigheads and others for safeguarding a few prime examples of wildland waterways were fulfilled and then surpassed. In 1980 President Jimmy Carter signed the Alaska National Interest Lands and Conservation Act, which put 97 million acres into new federal reserves. It tripled the amount in the National Wilderness Preservation System and doubled the size of the National Park System and of the National Wildlife Refuge System. The same legislation added 25 Alaskan rivers (33, counting tributaries) with a total of 3,284 miles to the WSR system, doubling its extent as well. All but seven of the 49th state's WSR additions already had a high level of protection by dint of being within one of the land reserves. For that matter, the 1,713,000-acre Yukon-Charley Rivers National Preserve was designed around pristine river courses and their watersheds.

As it happened, 1980 was a banner year for the national WSR system in general. California added 19 rivers with a total of 1,238 new miles. The Salmon WSR was extended by 125 miles in Idaho. Last but not least, 28 miles were tacked onto the 64 WSR miles of Ohio's Little Miami, the system's first urban-area river, designated in 1973.

During 1988 Oregon weighed in with a statewide omnibus bill mandating federal approval for a total of 1,442 miles along 44 rivers and 9 smaller tributaries. Four more waterways have been designated in Oregon since then, giving it by far the nation's largest WSR collection. Although this fits with the image of a rainy, stream-laced, environmentally conscious state, Oregon is also known for its timber industry.

Bob Doppelt, a former psychologist and river outfitter, founded the Oregon Rivers Council, a public-interest group instrumental in getting the Oregon Omnibus River Protection Bill passed. When we met a few years ago in the Eugene, Oregon, office of his conservation group, renamed the Pacific Rivers Council, he told me that large-scale logging and many other factors continued to threaten rivers and the species dependent upon them, despite the WSR system.

"Our salmon are disappearing at an alarming rate from rivers without a single dam," Doppelt said. "These fish are telling us that we can't save aquatic resources by protecting them in narrow corridors, and we can't do it as long as agencies keep addressing one commodity or one species or one issue at a time. We need management geared toward sustaining the health of the watershed as a whole."

His colleague, conservationist David Bayles, guided me toward the high, steep slopes of the Cascade Range. Being western Oregon, it was raining. I watched muddy sediments wash off freshly cleared logging sites and raw road cuts into headwater streams, silting over the gravel beds required by spawning fish. Other former breeding stretches were choked by woody logging debris or stripped of the streamside trees that once shaded and cooled them and kept the banks intact.

When we crossed a pass and descended into the drainage of the North Umpqua, Bayles said, "We had four of the five species of Pacific salmon running up here, along with steelhead (now classified as a sixth Pacific salmon species) and sea-run cutthroat trout. These days, the Umpqua's coho are in trouble, the pinks and chum are gone, and the sea-run cutthroat stock is at risk of extinction with the latest count down to 22 fish. And this is one of the most intact large salmon streams in the lower 48."

At the confluence of the North Umpqua and Steamboat Creek, Bayles told me, "Steamboat is the best stronghold of spring chinook and steelhead in the watershed. The Forest Service has proposed large clear-cuts on the very creeks that support those fisheries." As we continued alongside waters to which steelhead fishermen such as Ernest Hemingway and Zane Grey once made pilgrimages, a truck loaded with logs rumbled by. It was coming from the South Umpqua, already cut over and almost out of fish.

Bob Doppelt's critique of the WSR system's shortcomings seemed to make sense. What good does it do to declare one upstream fork of a river protected if other forks and the downstream portion are deteriorating? Why protect a quarter-mile-wide corridor along a WSR

RED RIVER *A natural greenway through Kentucky's Clifty Wilderness and Red River Gorge Geological*

Area, the Red River is inseparable from the lush Appalachian hardwood forests that outline its course.

section but permit logging to take place the length of a freshly toppled old-growth tree away from tributaries?

Yet the positive influence of the WSRA was becoming clearer to me at the same time. The act doesn't solve every problem or even most of them, but it focuses attention on rivers in important new ways. Rivers are all about continuity and connections. They naturally lead people to think in terms of watersheds, ecosystems, and biological diversity. WSR status provides a sort of scaffolding for further conservation efforts.

ONE NATIONAL ADVOCACY GROUP, the American Rivers Conservation Council, was formed in 1973 to enlarge and improve the WSR system. Known today simply as American Rivers, the organization works to protect riparian habitats, wetlands, and watersheds through a wide range of public policy initiatives as well. Its annual list of America's most endangered rivers is a reminder that the crisis that sparked the WSRA is far from over.

Don't forget all the smaller outfits that are dedicated to preserving and restoring a particular river basin or favorite little stream. By American Rivers's count, the U.S. holds about 3,500 such groups. There is probably one in your zip code area. They tend to have names like Possum Gulch River Alliance, Save The Little Big River Foundation, Citizens for Conodoguinit Creek, or Friends of the Wekiva River. Okay, I made up the first three names, though Pennsylvania does have a Conodoguinit Creek (my guess is that a dog can). As for the Friends of the Wekiva River, which winds north from the outskirts of Orlando, Florida, they saw more than a decade of endeavor bear fruit last year when 41.6 miles of the waterway and its tributaries became the second addition to the national WSR system in the new millennium.

The majority of those miles are in the wild category despite the fact that the area is rapidly being enclosed by suburban Orlando. Back in 1988 the state passed the Wekiva River Protection Act, a special measure unprecedented in Florida at the time, then began acquiring riverside property. By the time the Wekiva came up for final approval as a WSR, most of it was surrounded by public land—various state parks and reserves, a county park, Seminole State Forest, and acreage overseen by the St. Johns River Water Management District.

The real impetus for going to such lengths to preserve this sub-tropical river was the quality of its water. That liquid first appears rushing out of the earth in three major springs at a combined rate of about 90 million gallons per day and a constant temperature of about 70°F. The stuff took 17 years to get here, having been moving underground through 13-million-year-old phosphatic limestone during that time. And it is as clear as the finest crystal.

I'm floating just below Rock Springs at the moment, not in any kind of craft but in bathing trunks, breathing through a snorkel. Beyond my dive mask, the scene is so sharply outlined through the utterly transparent liquid that it reminds me of an illustration in a children's storybook about the underwater world—better than reality is supposed to look. And friendlier. Mr. Bass is here, hovering with Mr. Sunfish in the eelgrass. From under a ledge by the cattail stalks, Mr. Red-eared Turtle returns my stare while Mr. Water Beetle scoots to the surface to replenish his bright bubble of air.

Drifting like this feels a little like flying in slow motion. I continue for almost a quarter mile through Kelly Park, the small county reserve whose waters are visited by a thousand people daily when summer cranks up Florida's heat. After traipsing back upstream, I do it all over again. Then I paddle my kayak onto the Rock Springs Run of the Wekiva's main channel, tie the boat off to water lily stalks, and snorkel some more. The bass and bream are larger here. Otter tracks mark one shore. The vine-knit forest of sweet gum, live oak, and sabal palm is thicker and taller, closing overhead in places. A consideration intrudes: Hmmm, now where might Mr. Alligator be?

He—or she—appears several hundred yards, three white ibises, and a couple of great egrets downstream. Mr./Mrs. seven-foot reptile glides slowly across the channel, snout, eyes, and a couple of other scaly bumps just barely breaking the surface. By then, I'm back in the kayak. Gators aren't a real threat, but I prefer the foot-long mini-version sunning itself on a snag beside a gang of turtles. Although the Wekiva can be crowded with people some days, only two boats pass by this afternoon. I have all kinds of time to imagine myself on a largely unexplored continent, the way I feel canoeing the Missouri, the way it was not so very long ago when every river in North America was wild.

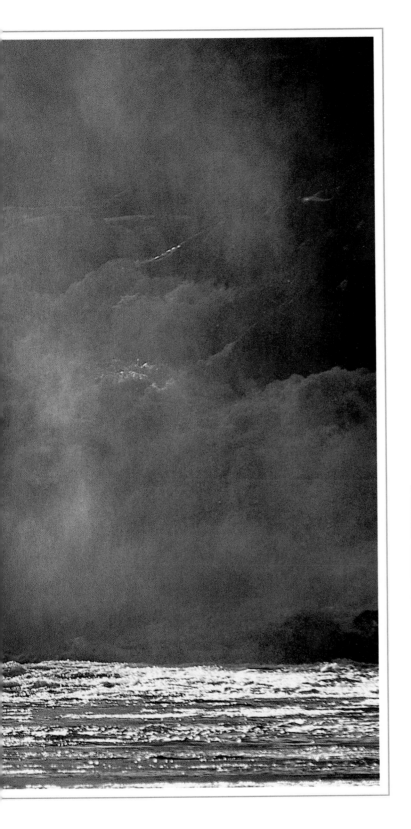

ALLAGASH RIVER

A proposed dam on the neighboring St. John River would have drowned Maine's Lower Allagash. Conservationists fought back that plan. Then, in 1965, Maine declared the Allagash a Wilderness Waterway. It was added to the National Wild and Scenic River system in 1970. So in the years ahead, boaters can continue to enjoy scenes like the raw power of Allagash Falls (left) next to delicate bunchberries (below) on the forest floor.

DELAWARE RIVER

Shared by Pennsylvania, New York, and New Jersey, the Delaware's 175.7 wild and scenic miles come in two sections, the Upper and the Middle, which flow through Delaware Water Gap National Recreation Area. Their corridors contain a variety of historic town sites, bridges, and farms dating back to America's youth. Considering its proximity to major East Coast cities, the river remains surprisingly undeveloped, which is one reason it still offers fine angling (below) for walleye, smallmouth bass, and spawning runs of shad coming home from the sea.

CHATTOOGA RIVER

As one river guide told the author, "I must have gone through Bull Sluice Rapids (below) a thousand times, and I still get butterflies in my stomach when I see it coming up." Tumbling off the Appalachians' southern end, the Chattooga passes through North and South Carolina as well as northeastern Georgia. While sections of it can be gut wrenching for the most experienced paddlers, other stretches are suitable for novices. And everyone—and her dog—can use the corridor for picnicking, hiking, and goofin' around on hot southern summer days.

LOXAHATCHEE RIVER Less than eight miles long, the protected part of this subtropical river is habitat for

the endangered manatee, but dikes, diversions, intensive farming, and urban expansion threaten its quality and flow.

WILD: As Grizzly as it Gets on the Noatak

In the language of the native Inupiat people, Noatak means "way to the interior."

Photographs by Raymond Gehman

For modern travelers, this Alaskan river is a way into a world yet untamed.

"...wild for as far as you can see and
ten times beyond that."

—RON YARNELL

A GRIZZLY HAS BEEN DIGGING for roots across the river ever since we made camp. On our side, bands of Dall sheep traverse the mountain behind us. But the thing we watch most closely is a stick that we planted upright at the edge of Alaska's Noatak River to mark its level. Our tents are pitched not far above, and the water is on the rise.

We're early. Or, rather, spring breakup is late this year, even for country above the Arctic Circle in Alaska's Brooks Range. Although this is the first week of June, the uplands remain snowbound. As we flew in by bush plane to land on this gravel bar near Twelvemile Creek, we could see that the Noatak was still cutting through its winter coat of ice for long stretches upstream.

Slab after white, slowly revolving slab comes drifting past camp on the rising meltwater, accompanied by clear chunks called candle ice that look like floating chandeliers. More ice is frozen to the river's bottom in luminous reefs. Downstream, the current sweeps up against bends lined by sharply undercut ice shelves, while a few channels remain almost completely blocked by ice bridges. We're

Wind, lapping waves, and summer's midnight sun etch patterns upon the Noatak's shore near Ledge Rapids (opposite). A feather (above) from old ptarmigan remains hints of lives gained and lost during the dark months of a winter that only recently yielded its grip on the land.

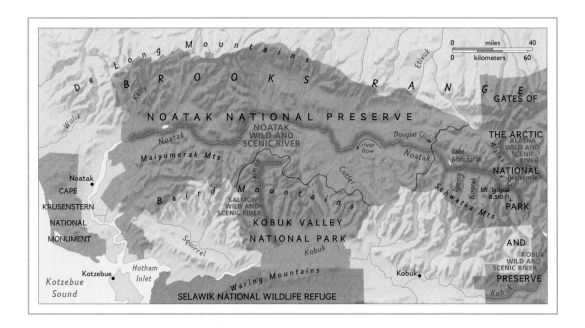

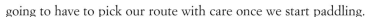

ALASKA

The Noatak flows from the central Brooks Range westward to the Chukchi Sea, keeping well above the Arctic Circle all the way. With 330 of its 396 miles designated as wild, this is the longest segment in America's national system of protected rivers.

going to have to pick our route with care once we start paddling.

First, though, we explore upriver. The permafrost underlying the tundra is beginning to melt on top, leaving the ground pocked with pools. Our feet are soon soaked and cold. The low-growing vegetation remains mostly brown and the willow branches bare, shivering in the wind. Spring seems a long way off. But as soon as we leave the marshy bottomlands and start up a steep, south-facing slope, the season of hope and renewal pokes its green head out of the hummocks to greet us.

Tender leaves are unfurling from the arctic bearberry, Lapland rosebay, and dwarf birch. I drop down to inspect the mat of tundra plants and instantly feel a bit warmer. Those thick, cushiony forms are designed for trapping solar heat to accelerate growth. In between rise packets of fertile color—the first wildflowers, attended by beetles and burly bumblebees.

Several hours farther up the sunward slope, we sprawl among sprouting fireweed and the petals of alpine avens to rest. Beside me and photographer Ray Gehman is 73-year-old C. Burton (Burt) Sharp, a wiry Virginian retired from the Defense Mapping Agency. This will be his first raft trip down a wild river but not because he lacks outdoor experience. After giving up marathon running, he turned to hiking and has traversed backcountry from the Appalachians to Nepal. "The general idea," he explains, "is to die young as late as possible."

The fourth and final member of our group, Ron Yarnell, guides for an expedition company called Arctic Wild. He has made trips to the Noatak for nearly three decades and come to know the lives of its resident plants and animals in intimate detail. Kneeling by one of the white bearberry blossoms dangling like elfin bells, he points out a ring of clear panes on its top, explaining, "That transparent part of the flower lets the sunlight penetrate to the interior, turning each bell into a miniature greenhouse."

I move the magnifying lens of my pocketknife over to a purple spike of lousewort flowers, then to the red catkin of a dwarf willow just two inches tall. Both turn out to be wrapped in fine, interwoven filaments that add a plush coat of insulation. When I look up, my eyes refocus on a tumult of snowbound peaks surrounding the 8,510-foot granite tooth called Mount Igikpak, highest summit in the central Brooks Range and the ultimate source of the Noatak.

That's the world north of tree line: intricate little adaptations that permit the tundra to flourish during its brief yearly encounter with heat amid raw panoramas almost too vast to take in. Other than some robust willows and the odd copse of cottonwoods, almost anything you see in the midsize range—taller than the tundra but smaller than a hill—is a warm-blooded animal. Like the silver wolf that watches us pass from a low rise above a slough. Or the moose that, catching the wolf's scent or ours, breaks into a trot in the distance.

"Time to think about heading back to camp before it gets dark," Yarnell announces. I'm fresh enough from the Lower 48 that I almost nod in agreement, until he adds, laughing, "We've only got about two months till then." At this latitude, the midnight sun might slip behind the mountains, but it won't give way to night until August. Still, it wouldn't hurt to eat dinner and sleep sometime before then. Sharp stands up in his soggy shoes, brushes leaves and old caribou droppings off the seat of his britches, adjusts a sweat-stained cap, and looks over the miles between us and our tents. "Right," he says. "What's a little pain when you're lookin' good?"

At camp, trying to spoon in bites before the wind off the river

Riding the light. The author steers a foldable canoe down the broad course

of the waterway, flowing with early June runoff from melting ice and snow.

makes my meal totally cold, I think: Tomorrow we join the flotilla of ice. Then, noticing the way the peaks are glowing, lit from below, I correct myself. Tomorrow is already here.

"You'll be the first party down the Noatak this year," said Glenn Hart, an Inupiat native and Park Service employee at the village of Bettles, when we checked in en route to Gates of the Arctic National Park and Preserve. "The park is about 8.4 million acres in size. From there, you'll float on into the Noatak National Preserve. It covers around 6.5 million acres and is bordered on the south by Kobuk Valley National Park, which is another couple of million acres." And, he could have added, just northeast of Gates of the Arctic lie the 19 million pristine acres of the Arctic National Wildlife Refuge.

As it nears the polar ocean, the Continental Divide bends west and heads across Alaska's northern rim. This is the Brooks Range, the

About half a million caribou from the Western Arctic herd pass through the Noatak basin twice every year. Striding easily across the spongy tundra and leftover snow on big, wide-spreading hoofs, they make their way to traditional spring calving sites on the North Slope of the Brooks Range. By midsummer, they are headed back south toward taiga wintering grounds with a new generation at heel.

northernmost major mountain system on the planet, and we're in its heart. Most of the region's rivers run down the North Slope to the ice-bound Beaufort Sea or south to eventually join the Yukon River. But the central Brooks Range splits into several chains, and the Noatak ends up flowing westward between the De Long and Baird Mountains to empty into the Chukchi Sea near Kotzebue.

In a few weeks, if not sooner, half a million caribou currently on their North Slope calving grounds will begin drifting back south through the Noatak Valley with new calves at their heels. Inupiat hunters used to follow the Western Arctic herd's migration across the river and on toward wintering sites; in their language, Noatak means "way to the interior." Some Inupiat stayed around the area to hunt and to fish for salmon, arctic char, and sheefish, or inconnu, a type of whitefish that can grow to more than ten feet long. After contact with

People often talk about contemplating the meaning of life. Some only kid about it. Others intend to get serious about making an effort one day. Geographer, world traveler, and veteran outdoorsman Burt Sharp of Virginia already has, in this instance while drifting in a raft during a Noatak journey that included the team from National Geographic.

whites, the native people moved downstream and became more settled. Today, the nearest community in the valley is the village of Noatak, more than 300 river miles downriver from our tents.

Five other national wild rivers originate within Gates of the Arctic National Park and Preserve: the Kobuk, which also flows westward, Alatna, John, Tinayguk, and North Fork of the Koyukuk. The latter was a favorite of Bob Marshall, the explorer, conservationist, and government official who bestowed the name Gates of the Arctic upon part of the Brooks Range during the 1930s. The park, in which only native subsistence hunting is allowed, and the Noatak Preserve, where sport hunting is permitted as well, were established as part of the sweeping Alaska National Interest Lands Conservation Act of 1980. All six rivers were designated at the same time.

The Noatak drains the largest watershed in the nation that has scarcely been touched by modern human influences. Nearly all of the 12,600-square-mile basin is recognized by the United Nations as an International Biosphere Reserve, a nature stronghold of global significance, offering opportunities for landscape-level studies of ecology, genetics, and the traditional use of resources by indigenous people. The river itself is the longest in any national reserve and the longest in the national wild and scenic river system, with 330 of its total of 396 miles protected. Given a setting this remote, it almost goes without saying that every one of those 330 WSR miles is classified as wild.

We break camp at Twelvemile Creek in the afternoon. Aiming downstream between patches of shore-fast ice with two of us paddling in the front of the 12-foot raft, two paddling in the rear, and a mammoth mound of gear monopolizing the rest of the craft, we pass tributaries pouring out of side valleys grander than some Lower 48 parks. They are crowned by mountains with more sets of mountains behind them, keeping the horizon in huge and lovely confusion.

If stretches of waterways such as the Missouri or central Arizona's Verde River qualify as wild, then the Noatak, along with some of the 25 other Alaskan rivers with WSR segments, almost deserves a separate category. Something on the order of extra jumbo wild or "wild for as far as you can see and ten times beyond that," to borrow the phrase Yarnell used to describe why he keeps coming here. Everything is so primeval, so freshly formed and unsullied, that we have a sense of being not just the earliest Europeans on the continent but perhaps the earliest humans, newly arrived across the Bering Strait.

"Back paddle, back paddle.... Now, spin right. Okay, we're good." As Yarnell keeps us aligned with the main current, I'm thinking that if the Noatak were much colder, grayer, or more laden with sediment, it would be permafrost. Instead, it is a 38-degree Fahrenheit ribbon of erosive power whose load of swirling grit sometimes makes a hissing sound against our blades. The afternoon is warm, and the water rises steadily, gathering speed. Banks of frozen soil begin collapsing and slide into the flow. Ice walls whomp loose like calving mini-glaciers. Half-submerged floes bump along the raft's underside. Some of the tributaries have spilled over their ice dams and are cutting new channels through the tundra en route to join the surge. By the time we pull in to make camp, the river is seething.

Along with rock ptarmigan, the Brooks Range hosts willow ptarmigan like this one in transition from white winter plumage to summer brown. The birds change footwear to match the season as well. With the onset of winter, their toes sprout dense feathers and grow longer claws. The combination quadruples the surface that distributes the birds' weight on snow, much as snowshoes serve north country humans.

Oxbow lakes, the remains of former channels, accompany the Noatak on its way through the big

valley roughed out by ice age glaciers and continuously redesigned by the river's meandering flow.

Caribou shed their antlers annually. Rodents such as lemmings obtain scarce minerals by gnawing the fallen racks. Meanwhile, the roots of alpine avens (below, top) and wooly lousewort (below, bottom) conduct their own search for nutrients in the shallow layer of summer-thawed soil above the permafrost.

With only the briefest
of respites from winter,
the headwaters of the
Noatak invoke the
Pleistocene epoch, when
much of the world's fresh
water stayed locked up
as white crystals.

Sometime the next morning—I've consigned my watch to a gear bag—we ferry across the Noatak for a mountainside hike. Bachelor bands of Dall sheep rams and much larger groups of ewes with subadults and brand new lambs dot the slopes like pockets of leftover snow. The animals keep a wary eye on us but are content to stay at a distance rather than flee altogether, possibly because they haven't been hunted. One bunch of females and young descends to a bare patch that appears to be a mineral lick. While some nibble at the soil, subadults take turns sparring head-to-head, and other animals break into downhill dances, whirling in clouds of dust.

We sit among silvery lichens and rock jasmine flowers on the next set of cliffs to watch the sheep show and the golden eagles soaring by in search of arctic ground squirrels. Yet the real spectacle is simply the setting. Below, in the immense corridor of the Noatak Valley, framed by rows of peaks, the shining river loops back and forth with oxbow lakes set like parentheses along its course. Most are frozen, and they glisten even more brightly than the river in the passing storm light between streaks of rain.

More mixed skies await us the following morning. According to what must be some cosmic law, we no sooner take the tents' rain flies off and have all our gear exposed, spread out to be packed, than the rain gets serious. We still have to put together our canoe, a bundle of waterproof fabric stretched over aluminum ribs. Since we're safely through the worst of the ice, I'm to take this boat from here on. A deluge hits almost the instant we launch. The gusts that come with it sail my high-riding vessel toward roiling waters beneath an undercut bank. Before I slam into trouble, I turn the heavy end, the stern, straight into the crosswind and stroke hard in reverse and thus proceed on my maiden voyage bobbing sideways down the Noatak while paddling backwards.

The upper river is nearly all Class I and II water, fairly easy to navigate under ordinary conditions. Once the gusts let off a bit and I load more heavy bags in the bow and can actually steer, the route is a lot more enticing. I wouldn't go so far as to relax, though. The water is running too high and wide. And too cold; if you dumped, you wouldn't have long to get to shore before your muscles quit working. I'm almost hypothermic as it is. The wind and rain continue, and the air temperature is steadily dropping.

Below the confluence with a tributary called the Kugrak River, we tie the boats at the mouth of a small, clear, gravel-bottomed creek and walk around to warm up and stretch. Bear trails and old piles of dung pattern the banks, for chum salmon run up the stream to spawn later in summer. Two men hiking this way from the Kugrak ran into a grizzly in the willow brush, Yarnell recalls. One man came out alive.

To put the tale in perspective, Gates of the Arctic gets about 1,200 to 1,500 visitors annually. Although nobody counts exactly how many travel the Noatak, the estimate is around 200 each year, making this a lightly used river by most standards but the most heavily used one in the Brooks Range. The Kugrak encounter is the sole record of a fatality from grizzlies in this part of the park and preserve.

Just the same, I strap on my holster with its spray canister of red-pepper bear deterrent when I hike out from our evening camp near the incoming Igning River, sloshing through a cotton grass sedge marsh toward two shallow lakes. The closest one has thawed. Its waters bustle with aquatic invertebrates, green-winged teal, red-breasted mergansers, and two types of nesting waterfowl that spend the rest of the year at sea: oldsquaw ducks and surf scoters. The larger lake is mostly ice, with one open lead. What I take to be small bergs floating in it become tundra swans in my binoculars. The flurries of white shards around them are arctic terns diving for food.

Another day, another battle with head winds whenever the river swings into them, and another evening session of lugging gear from the boats up to a campsite with bear spray strapped on my hip. It's impossible not to think about grizzlies when the tundra holds signs wherever we walk. The big omnivores gravitate to these mountains from a wide region to take advantage of certain conditions, advanced spring growth being a prime example.

While the bear diggings around me now look like last year's, stak-

ing down your tent between divots raked out by long claws does nothing to calm the imagination. Raven calls draw my attention toward the south-facing cliffs just uphill from camp. The sun is backlighting something the color of dried grass. How we all missed this during an earlier look around, I don't know, because it happens to be a grizzly snoozing on a ledge. And, uh, yeah, a second one lies not far away.

I hope the two are a female and cub. Out of concern for her offspring, a mother is unlikely to boldly approach strange doings from a distance. But when the second bear turns, I can see that it is roughly the same size. We've got a mating pair or else two grown siblings off on their own—adolescents.

Their beds are maybe 300 yards from where we plan to sleep. What next? There's a good chance that they have never encountered people before, and four of us is a fairly imposing number. On the other hand, we're packing along stores of food and a smelly, growing bag of garbage. The nearest tree tall enough to climb or hang our edibles in is hundreds of miles distant. Yarnell says he is comfortable staying put but that we might have a wakeful night ahead. Eventually, we arrive at a group decision. It is: Why take a chance? We strike the tents, tote the

Led by guide Ron Yarnell, Burt Sharp and the author hike from their first campsite, near Twelvemile Creek, up toward a view of the Noatak's ultimate source, 8,510-foot Mount Igikpak.

The Geographic party was likely the first to run the upper Noatak after the ice breakup in 2001. They met hundreds of Dall sheep, bands of musk oxen, half a dozen moose, nearly as many grizzlies, and no Homo sapiens.

bags back down to the boats, and lash them in, ready to shove off. Ahhh. Now we can watch at our leisure.

Minutes later, the grizzlies are up. They are beautiful beasts in sumptuous coats, one light gold with chocolate feet, the other a more silvery blond. Each tests the air a while before it begins feeding uphill. One gets well ahead of the other, which lopes after it. When they reunite, they rise up snarling and cuff one another, play-fighting. This is the first pair of cavorting grizzlies that Sharp has seen. He is clearly impressed. We all

are—and hike up a rise to keep them in view a while longer.

Several long river bends farther, my paddling muscles are talking to me about too much overtime. But as Sharp says, what's a little pain when you're lookin' good? Check it out: I'm wearing sunglasses at midnight, dealing with the glare off the river. After dinner at our second camp of the evening, I dig out my watch: 2:22 a.m., a good time to stroll up the nearby bluff for a view.

In the rich light of the wee hours, the tundra flares gold as a grizzly's coat, and I reflect anew upon riding a swollen river through back-of-beyond country where great bears run the show. The place may get busier with floaters later in the season, but the magnitude of wildness will still humble each one, and then winter will return to wipe away the traces of all. Winter lingers in the wind off the peaks even now. Back by my tent, I find a bag that got wet in the canoe slick with fresh ice.

If you've camped wearing a woolen hat day after day, you know how grand it feels to finally wash your itchy head. I lather up around mid-morning, taking advantage of the sunshine beating into our cubbyhole at the base of the bluff. The day warms enough that I'm even swatting at mosquitoes. Briefly. Within half an hour, the cold wind is back. Clouds thicken. Some are already in turmoil over the peaks.

"We get two fronts here: warm southern air from the coast and a high, dry Arctic air mass, and they battle it out over the Brooks Range," says Yarnell as we set off toward the mountains on another hike. Our route follows the ridge of a moraine left by ice age glaciers.

In the land of round-the-clock light, the dinner stove may come out at noon or in the wee hours of morning. Paddling sessions and hikes are scheduled according to rainstorms, winds, and curious bears rather than by the clock.

Since water percolates quickly through this giant gravel deposit, the upper portion stays fairly dry. We're not the only ones that like to travel such slopes. We pass a wolf den, fox tracks, and evidence of the canines' hunts—patches of white ptarmigan feathers and weathered bones—along with the grizzly diggings and shed caribou antlers that by now seem typical of the Noatak countryside.

Over the miles since our headwaters camp, the valley has widened considerably, and it takes a while to reach its cliffy sides. A familiar scene emerges, with golden eagles patrolling slopes where Dall sheep graze. I climb to a high point above a sleeping ram, bundle up against the wind, and take a nap myself. Afterward, as we cross a saddle, yet another grizzly monopolizes our attention. The bear is distant but headed our way at a fairly good clip. There is no group discussion this time. We just turn and start down the mountainside.

As we near the base of the sheep cliffs, the bear reverses direction and angles downslope, having caught the scent from three rams bedded upwind. But the bear cuts back too far. By the time it breaks into a run, the rams have smelled danger and are on the move. The chase is halfhearted. Without surprise on its side, the grizzly can only hope for a sheep too ill or injured to keep up with the others. When none fail the running test, the bear turns to sniffing a pile of boulders and begins to dig after ground squirrels.

We spend much of the next day on shore waiting out powerful winds before finally moving onto the river. Although the valley continues to widen, we get a tour of both sides, because the Noatak keeps swinging back and forth as though reluctant to lose touch with either of the mountain ranges that enclose it. Near Lake Matcharak, we call it a day and hope for a break in the churning weather.

No luck. When we board the boats in the morning, the winds are as strong as ever, and the uplands are white with fresh snow. We put some miles in our wake anyway and break for lunch in a swale behind a high river bluff. The site is a natural solarium, its warm, sandy soil cloaked with grass and the pink blossoms of wild vetch. Away from the rush of river and wind, white-crowned sparrow songs ring out from the willows. It isn't as though we're always paying attention to flora and fauna on this journey. We discuss politics, religion, other travels,

River bar, 3:00 a.m.: Though near freezing, the sky and waterway often seem to

smolder like embers for hours on end as sunset gives way directly to sunrise.

great meals we have met, and whether or not Gehman took more than his share of dessert again. It's just that in such a big, unpeopled landscape, the wildlife seems to become part of your social circle.

Sometimes termed a wasteland or barren grounds, the Arctic strikes me as more of an uncluttered stage for the drama of natural history. If it's a wasteland, why are we traipsing through wildflowers on our way toward sheep or away from grizzlies half the time? If it's barren, why do I see not only golden eagles but peregrine falcons almost every day? Why do the countless tundra pools and lakes produce such a bounty of insects that birds converge upon these teeming wetlands to reproduce? In addition to swimmers from swans to loons, the Noatak Valley draws wheatears from Africa, wagtails from Asia, golden plovers from the South Pacific, and arctic terns all the way from Antarctica. In places, every other step through ordinary looking tundra flushes a ground-nesting longspur or lark.

Paddling onward, we enter a wide, braided segment of the river. Two musk oxen loom among the shoreline willows. Massive and helmet-horned, they appear to have shambled straight out of the ice age. Three more appear farther downstream, shedding strips of their long, shaggy outer hairs and fine woolen underfur in preparation for summer. All but wiped out during the era of early contact with whites and firearms, the species was reintroduced to the Arctic National Wildlife Refuge during the 1970s. The herds have been expanding to reclaim swaths of their former range.

Barren wastes? Hardly. Bitter cold and squally? Absolutely, and worse by the minute. I wish I had a musk ox's coat. Paddling against the wind in one strand of a braided section, I find my boat being blown back upstream, and we still have half of our day's goal of 30 miles to cover. Who cares? We are completely on our own, out of radio contact, so thoroughly disconnected from environments molded to suit human needs that to get frustrated by a schedule no longer makes any sense. Hey, it's just weather.

We set up a tent and hunker down to wait for a lull. It comes toward evening. At Douglas Creek, we cross the invisible line separating Gates of the Arctic park from the Noatak Preserve. The next miles, floated after midnight, lead into a canyon where the Noatak

Summer tundra turns extra soggy where water collects from snow melting above the surface and permafrost melting below. Countless lakes fill low-lying areas, grading into sedge-strewn marshes that play host to a variety of nesting waterfowl.

slices through a series of thick terminal moraines. Despite the low air temperatures, the river is still running high. It accelerates between the high walls and builds standing waves that break over the gunwales as I bounce through. Ahead are Ledge Rapids, where a sudden drop sets up a series of back-curling waves that could easily swamp me. I eddy out above their roar, and that is where we camp for two nights, exploring the nearby lakes and hills.

Before the last full day of floating, I break down the canoe and add it and myself to the raft's load. There are small rapids nearly the whole way, including one set that opens a whirlpool under the nose of

the boat as we squirt around a sharp bend. The following day, the pilot of the floatplane that arrives to pick us up chooses to land on the river some distance downstream, so we have one more piece of the Noatak to run after all. I savor that final mile.

The end of our trip coincides with the end of the moraines. We have covered less than a third of the WSR portion of the Noatak. Had we continued downstream, we would have found the valley broadening until the mountains become distant backdrops, and we probably would have run into caribou returning from the North Slope. I got used to seeing these northernmost members of the deer family when I hiked the Sheenjek and Hulahula Rivers during other trips to the Brooks Range. Once, I kayaked the Kongakut River down to Caribou Pass and intercepted the Porcupine herd, 110,000 animals strong. On the Noatak, we came upon thousands of migration trails etched into the tundra but only a single caribou, and Gehman and I found that one in pieces, cached under a pile of vegetation by a grizzly.

I gaze out the window of the plane as it lifts off, content to think of the Western Arctic herd on its way with a new generation of fawns. Yarnell taps me on the shoulder. He is pointing out the window on the opposite side. There, maybe five miles on down from our last camp, a caribou band stands near a river wild for as far as you can see and ten times beyond that.

Paddle power meets propeller power as the raft team makes the final strokes of the voyage. After loading gear onto the floatplane, they will briefly ride the Noatak once more, since the river serves as the runway.

Vast as it is, the Noatak valley is but one of many along Alaska's northern rim. Carried on currents through such an

immense, unspoiled realm, you can scarcely help but take a parallel journey to places deep within the heart and mind.

SCENIC: Of Time, the Desert, and the Rio Grande

On America's third-longest river, rafters ride the border between

Photographs by Raymond Gehman

Texas and Mexico, shadow and sunlight, tranquility and adventure.

*"Rivers are the ultimate metaphor for life.
In their wake, they provide nourishment for
forests, wildlife, and people....
Without healthy rivers, we are lost."*

—Ian Kean

URING THE 19TH CENTURY, a group of Spanish gold-seekers was probing far upstream along what the conquistadores before them called the Río Bravo del Norte (Big River of the North), when they were attacked by Indians. The men escaped on a raft, but Francisco Torres, the priest among them, lay mortally wounded. Drifting onward, he looked up to see the last light of his last day on Earth caught atop a range of 13,000- and 14,000-foot peaks, glowing bright crimson. To Father Torres, it was as if the blood of Christ were washing down from the heavens. And that is how the Sangre de Cristo Mountains got their name.

I'm climbing along their base amid heaps of pure sand 700 feet tall. To the west, across the San Luis Valley, rise Colorado's San Juan Mountains, the birthplace of the Big River, el Rio Grande. For ages, the waters poured off those slopes, carrying their volcanic debris and spreading the sediments around a shifting floodplain on the valley floor. Winds picked up the grains and tossed them eastward, gust by gust, until they hit the Sangre de Cristo range and collected in the piles that are now Great Sand Dunes National Monument and Preserve.

The upper San Luis Valley stands 8,000 feet above sea level. Its winds

High above heat-cracked river mud (above) and sunbaked cliffs, lechuguilla plants, characteristic of the Chihuahuan Desert, send forth towers of flowers (opposite). Like other members of the agave family such as sotol, fermented to make mescal, and century plants, lechuguilla may grow and collect scarce water for 15 to 30 years or even longer before finally producing its massive bloom.

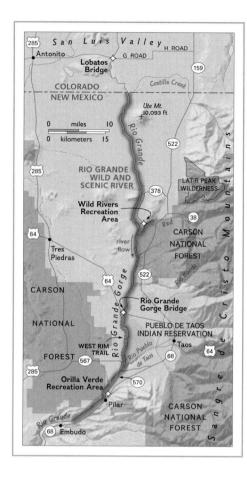

The Rio Grande is born among peaks of the San Juan Mountains in Colorado, 1,885 miles from its mouth. Upon entering New Mexico, it is designated as a wild and scenic river for the next 64 miles (above). Texas' Big Bend region (opposite) holds a second wild and scenic river section, which runs for 191 miles through limestone canyons as deep as 1,800 feet.

aren't bringing sand today. They are carrying fine snow. The Rio Grande now roams along the western side of the valley in a channel less than 100 feet from shore to shore. I walk across it on solid ice. Farther down the valley, frozen irrigation canals lead off both sides, and where the river passes through the town of Alamosa, it is striped with snowmobile tracks.

When Americans hear the name Rio Grande, many picture a hot, flat sprawl of desert. They see a wide, muddy river that Apaches, Mexican armies, *bandidos*, Texas Rangers, and cowboys whooping at longhorn cattle rode through. For better or worse, people also think of an international border swum by so many illegal immigrants that its waters contributed to the derogatory name wetback. The Rio Grande fits those descriptions, but only in places. This is the third-longest waterway in the U.S. As it winds 1,885 miles from its source to the delta where it dissolves into the Gulf of Mexico, the Big River offers more different scenes and moods than most of us could imagine.

After the Rio Grande crosses from Colorado into New Mexico, it becomes a Wild and Scenic River (WSR) for the next 64 miles. Moving more than fast enough to stay ice free, it hurries down a gorge cut from hills clad in junipers and piñons, churning through rapids that people run in the warm months, pounding over falls that the boats have to be toted around. Springs add to the flow, and it is clear enough in summer that trout populations thrive, luring fly fishermen from afar.

Southward, the hills smooth out onto the Taos Plateau, but the water doesn't. It keeps dropping as the gorge deepens until the Rio Grande is 850 feet below the rest of the landscape, locked within nearly vertical walls of dark basalt. I'm not tempted to test the early February waters jumping around down there. But I can go almost ten miles hovering over them like a golden eagle—or at least feeling as if I were—by hiking a trail along the canyon's western rim.

I wander away from the precipice, following coyote prints in lingering patches of snow. The Rio Grande and its abrupt gorge vanish so quickly from view that they may as well have been an illusion. Yet I am still well within the WSR corridor, and when antelope tracks lead me back toward a viewpoint, I eat lunch with the green-and-white water once again straight down past the toes of my boots.

Together with river campsites and recreation areas, the trail is maintained by the Bureau of Land Management, which oversees this section of the Rio Grande and four WSR miles of a tributary, the Red River. It does the same for 24.6 WSR miles of New Mexico's Rio Chama, which joins the Rio Grande farther downstream. In all, the bureau manages 34 designated rivers in 5 states that contribute roughly 20 percent of the total mileage in the national system.

Below the WSR stretch, the Rio Grande gentles. Its gorge gives way to rolling countryside, and diversions for agriculture reappear along with dams. The frontiersmen following tales of gold and other treasure in the region had no idea that the stuff in their drinking cups would one day prove to be the most precious commodity hereabouts. Consumers in Colorado already pump so much water out of the Rio Grande some years that the level in the New Mexico WSR section drops too low to float in places. Then New Mexico itself and northern Texas take their turns bleeding the waterway dry.

The Rio Grande defines 1,250 miles of the U.S.-Mexico border. Yet for the first 250, from El Paso to the Texas town of Presidio, the riverbed often holds little but sun-cracked mud and dust. It is restored to life by its chief tributary, the Rio Conchos, which comes out of

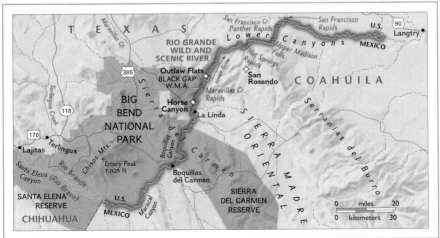

While traveling the Lower Canyons below Big Bend National Park, boaters

take advantage of a break in the steep rock walls to explore the desert beyond.

Mexico's Sierra Madre Oriental Range and drains an area almost as large as the U.S. share of the Rio Grande watershed.

Farther downstream, the river makes a southward swing and runs by 300,000-acre Big Bend Ranch State Park, 801,000-acre Big Bend National Park, and Texas' Black Gap Wildlife Management Area, with its newly restored population of desert bighorn sheep, and then by a series of remote, sparsely inhabited ranches. The opposite shore adjoins the Santa Elena Reserve in Mexico's state of Chihuahua and the Sierra del Carmen Reserve in the state of Coahuila. This is an enormous coalition of wild and scenic country, where peaks and plateaus 8,000 feet high drop more than a mile in altitude into Chihuahuan Desert ravines. Surely any river running through the heart of it all would be wild and scenic as well. In 1978, 191.2 Rio Grande miles here were formally declared to be just that, with the Park Service as the lead management agency.

The first 64 miles are the southern edge of Big Bend National Park. They pass through three monumental canyons whose sidewalls tower 1,800 feet above the water. Below the park, the Rio Grande enters more gorges that, while not always as deep, are continuous for most of the next 127 WSR miles. A journey down that stretch, called the Lower Canyons, is an immersion in geology with spiritual overtones.

Come along if you like. A party is already assembling, led by Ian Kean, a brawny river outfitter who, I'm told, is given to singing old boatmen's ballads around the evening fire until even the bats and owls start nodding off. His company, called the River League, based in Vancouver, British Columbia, operates partly as a business and partly to promote the conservation of unspoiled waterways, mainly in western Canada and Alaska. The Rio Grande is Kean's annual winter venture. This one includes five other guides and a dozen clients, counting myself and my daughter, Teal. While that may not sound like a recipe for desert solitude, Teal and I have our own kayaks. We plan to rendezvous with the group each night but otherwise need make only occasional contact with the league's three big, poky rafts during the 12 days we will be out.

I'm not sure what kind of company the river itself will be. All I know is that there are few ways in or out of the Lower Canyons once you commit, and they hold occasional whitewater up to Class III, the type one guidebook defines as: "Difficult—long rapids with powerful or irregular

waves, rocks, eddies; requires precise maneuvering, mandatory scouting."

Hoping to get some sense of what lies ahead, I check out the entrance to Boquillas, longest of the three canyons in the national park. A small village of the same name overlooks the Rio Grande from the Mexican side. To get there from the park, you signal a group of entrepreneurs waiting on the opposite shore with horses and burros. No, they don't come galloping across. They row over in a leaky dinghy and then, for a couple more dollars, rent you one of the animals to ride to town.

Boquillas's inhabitants used to grow extensive gardens on the floodplain to supply local miners. These days, their main business appears to be selling curios and drinks to thirsty visitors. It's a pleasant but unremarkable place. The same could be said of the Rio Grande crossing, though I notice that the current has a bit more tug than the water's flat surface would suggest.

So I drive around to the downstream end of Boquillas Canyon, the launch site for our trip. I've arranged to meet Andy Kurie there at another small outpost, Heath Canyon Ranch, across from La Linda, Mexico, and ask this longtime resident's opinion of what to expect from the river. He leads me to an old bridge, closed off after

Kayakers who ride the Lower Canyons' Rodeo Rapids sideways come mighty close to getting bucked off.

it became a funnel for contraband. The bottom of the span is about 35 feet above the Rio Grande.

Kurie says, "When the river floods, the irrigated truck farms get washed out upstream. One time, we were watching waves of onions and cantaloupes go by when here comes a house roof with a guy on top of it. Doggone if he wasn't asleep. He must have had some rough times through the canyons. We started yelling at him because we thought he might get scraped off against the bottom of the bridge. When he woke up, he just smiled and waved at us and went right on. I've seen the river rise within three feet of the bridge two other times. Seen it when it was just sand, too, and a few pools in the shady parts."

According to the gauge on the bridge, the river is currently just three-and-a-half feet deep, nowadays more or less normal for the end of February, Kurie informs me. After his story, I'm thinking: normal is good. Give me unremarkable. Give me peaceful currents with a bit of a tug. We'll worry about what they do at the rapids when we reach them.

By the afternoon of our first day on the water, I'm even thinking that it might be okay if my boat flips over in white water. The temperature is in the 90s, and I'm stopping for a swim every half-hour or so anyway. Rains heavy enough to break a several-year drought have been sweeping through all winter. Cononsequently, this onset of spring heat is restyling the spare desert floor with extraordinarily plush wall-to-rock-wall flower carpeting—Big Bend bluebonnet, bicolor mustard in blue and white, a yellow sunflower called desert baileya, and clusters of purple nama. Flower buds are emerging on the prickly pear cactuses, and big blossoms that look like cream-colored banana clusters have shot up from the yuccas.

Like the yuccas, a variety of desert species follow the strategy of blooming only once every few years, and it looks as if they all decided that this is absolutely the year. The slopes are rainbowed with petals, the air cross-threaded with strange, sweet fragrances. Purling along to its own tune, the waterway runs tan as silt or cliff reflections one moment, sky-colored the next, then green as the cane thickets lining its shores. And the paddling is easy. Except for a couple of cholla cactus spines in my leg from a walk—I'd forgotten that the desert has other ways of commanding your attention—I'd declare a perfect start.

We camp just past Horse Canyon and arise the next morning to daybreak-tinged rimrock and cardinals singing in the cane. They look like more of the scarlet blossoms lining the riverside. Black phoebes perch on stalks bent out from the shores and wing low over the water to catch insects. Midges, which live most of their lives as aquatic larvae, have emerged to form mating swarms so dense that they resemble mist rising from the currents. Higher up, red-tailed hawks and Chihuahuan ravens ride the first thermals, and a peregrine falcon watches us pass from a canyonside perch.

I rejoin the rafters around noon, and we walk up toward an overhanging cliff to escape the sun. Ironically, another sun greets us right there. It was etched into the rock next to the symbol of a snake by one of the native cultures that hunted and cultivated the river's shores. The earliest arrived at least 10,000 years before our lunchtime break. Toward evening we hit the first tumbling water, Maravillas Creek Rapids—an easy ride at this water level—and pitch our tents at the start of Outlaw Flats.

Rounding a bend the next day I suddenly come upon horses tied in the brush and two Mexicans sitting on the bank with poles in their hands, waiting for catfish to bite. With the current pulling me on down the fish highway, we barely have time to exchange a *buenos dias*. Evening finds me up toward the rimrock in their nation, looking back

Lunching while adrift, outfitter Ian Kean of the River League takes a break from the oars, flanked by guides Susan Francis (with head scarf) and Ursula Schmitt. Francis, a scuba diving instructor back home in Vancouver, British Columbia, also teaches yoga, a good way to limber up after hours of sitting aboard a raft.

In the wake of drought-breaking rains, the blossoms of countless long-dormant plants suddenly turn the Chihuahuan Desert lush, fragrant, and rainbow-colored. Here (left), purple nama and the white stalks of bicolor mustard rise next to one of several species of prickly pear cactus common in the region. Perhaps the easiest to identify is the purple-tinged prickly pear (below), which can assume the hue of a Texas sunset.

into Texas. (By agreement, visitors to this WSR may camp on either side and wander a modest distance into Mexico without having to obtain special permission.) The two sides are identical, a single geological and biological unit briefly interrupted by running water.

One of the signatures of this ecosystem is the plant called lechuguilla. Its dagger leaves form thickets that force you and your ankles to constantly re-route during a stroll. It is a member of the agave family, sometimes termed century plants, many of which may wait 15 years or longer before blossoming. But when they do, they go all out. The stalk that shoots forth from the center bears a chandelier of flowers that dwarfs the rest of the foliage.

The dominant bush around me is creosote. It produces a toxic compound that keeps other plants at bay, creating a circle of largely barren ground around each bush. The creosote's roots can then monopolize whatever fickle rainfall hits those few square yards. When

The Chihuahuan Desert is the easternmost of four distinctly different desert biomes found in North America. Nearly overwhelmed by the variety of vegetation on display following a wet winter, river guides James Wigmore and Susan Francis try to identify species.

a creosote blooms, its yellow flowers draw more than 100 species of bees. Most are semi-solitary desert specialists that dwell in underground burrows, and more than 20 are so dependent upon the bush that they time their emergence to coincide with its blossoming. The rest of the plant remains noxious-tasting. However, insects being little chemical factories in their own right, two species, a grasshopper and a walkingstick, have figured out how to break down the toxic compounds, and they dine on nothing but creosote leaves.

Another plant typical of this landscape is termed little candle—*candelia*—for the wax cuticle on its stalks. The coating is to seal precious moisture in. Since water can evaporate from leaves more readily, the little candle doesn't produce any—just stems or stalks from its basal root. People still gather the plant, especially in Mexico, and render its wax for use in everything from shoe polish and cosmetics to insulation.

I'm starting to believe that the real natural wonder here is not so much the river with its canyons as it is the Chihuahuan Desert with its remarkably adapted life-forms. The Rio Grande is more like a splendid portal into it. As the sun sets across the canyons, deepening the flower rug's colors, feeding the shadows that wait in thousands of caves along the limestone cliffs, slowly yielding to the night creatures whose tracks I've been seeing in the river mud—bobcats, beavers, raccoons, and possibly their long-tailed relatives, coatimundi—I feel I could happily wander this wet seam in the drylands for weeks. Another day of paddling and probing can't begin too soon....

All right, it can. My journal for February 28 reads roughly as follows: Please don't send me out on that old river this morning, boss. I was awakened after midnight when the weird, sultry air that moved in after sundown gave way to a tent-flapping windstorm. And it was a cold one, a real blue norther that sent stuff cartwheeling all over camp: storage sacks, folding chairs, hats left by the smoldering fire, loose life jackets, and I don't know what else I chased down by flashlight and anchored with rocks. My eyes are still full of grit. I've got on a wool hat and every piece of clothing I brought, but my toes are turning purple in my river sandals. I'm dreading the first rapid because my open kayak always ships a little water over the side if I hit a wave sideways. I can picture my wet butt turning the same color as my toes—all too

The River League expedition camps at Asa Jones Hot Springs. Hidden within the giant cane that edges the Rio

Grande, the bathtub-temperature stream is one of many issuing from the base of the river's limestone ramparts.

clearly. No sir, if winter is coming out of retirement, I don't want to go.

In the first part of the Lower Canyons, a rutted road leads to the shore. After that come a couple of abandoned shacks and a sporadically used fishing camp. They are reminders that the Texas side is privately owned ranch land, which is why this lengthy segment of the river is classified scenic rather than wild. Nevertheless, it is one of the loneliest outbacks in the entire lower 48 states, more secluded overall than the officially wild park segment. And, wouldn't you know, when the sky is low and brooding, trailing sketches of rain, this is the day the Lower Canyons noticeably deepen. Strong headwinds funnel between the ramparts, carrying harsh whispers and the echoes of bird cries, and they make distant rapids sound louder, as though we are almost upon them.

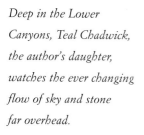

Deep in the Lower Canyons, Teal Chadwick, the author's daughter, watches the ever changing flow of sky and stone far overhead.

On an afternoon ramble to shake off the chill of the voyage, I follow a wash far up the Mexican slopes. The grade steepens, and I have to climb headwalls, then crawl beneath truck-size boulders fallen off the cliffsides to rest precariously atop one another in the ravine. A side

gully holds a ledge full of resurrection plants. They can persist in a brown, dead-looking state for months or occasionally years until they collect enough moisture to turn green and unfurl. The latest round of showers has provided it—a hopeful sign. But I am not buoyed by it. Instead, a vaguely unsettled feeling spreads from my stomach to the back of my neck.

Perhaps it's only the incongruity of this cold pall over a desert where the temperature spikes above 100°F almost every day for five months of the year. The sky has gone as gray as its stone canyon frame, and a stone pillar or yucca plant silhouetted against the gloomy clouds will suddenly seem to take on human form, becoming a strange, silent sentinel. Booga-booga-booga; what the heck is wrong with me? I'm about two degrees shy of declaring the place haunted, when I come upon the dried mud of a temporary pool that had formed in the wash. In its center is the large paw print of *un gato muy grande*—one very big cat.

Puma: the possibility had already flashed through my mind as the wash narrowed to ambush dimensions. There are certainly enough javelina and deer around to support mountain lions, and I've been wondering how long the odd stray horse or band of cows that makes its way down into the canyon lasts. In a way, finding the track is almost a relief. It gives me something solid to pin my worries upon, not to mention a convenient excuse to turn back a little sooner than planned. I'd rather lurk beside the crew fixing dinner and pounce on appetizers myself.

For the remainder of the journey, a succession of weather fronts swirling in from the west leaves us shivering one day and sweating the next. Happily, the Rio Grande offers warm springs at intervals along the shores. They soak away not only the cold but the fine mud-bank sediments that have come to impregnate every fabric and pore over the days. Some of the springs feeding the river nurture populations of endangered desert pupfish, much as the river itself is home to a turtle found nowhere else, the Big Bend slider. It is also a stronghold for the rare blue sucker, a stout fish that favors the swiftest sections of rapids.

Only for the briefest of moments do I give the finned residents any thought as I slalom through Hot Springs Rapids, Upper Madison Falls, Panther Rapids, San Francisco Rapids, and their like. I'm far too absorbed in trying to stay upright. Sometimes, I no sooner get past than

I need to walk back upstream and find footing in the torrent so I can help lift the rafts over boulders too close together for the big boats to shoot between. Yet for every mad dash or half-hour of heaving, there will be long, calm spells of drifting past newly leafed oaks, Berlandier ash, and Mexican buckeye trees with luxuriant pink flower sprays; for every headwind, a gyre of turkey vultures riding invisible eddies, or the sudden, jeweled flight of a green kingfisher between shores.

At his office in Big Bend National Park, Rio District ranger Marcos Paredes, who coordinates management of the WSR, told me that 1,300 people annually float the Rio Grande in the Lower Canyons. Many more of them go with a commercial outfitter farther upstream, usually on a short trip through a segment in the park. "It's possible to go a week in the Lower Canyons and not see a soul," he said. "To me, that's one of the river's greatest natural values; hard to measure but an incredible resource. To protect it, we may limit the number of parties allowed to float at any given time."

Probably not anytime soon. We are alone for almost a week before we meet a Mexican family from a ranch called San Rosendo. One of them, who introduces himself as Antonio, tells me that the two men I saw fishing days earlier were from the same outfit, which runs cattle and offers private hunting on about 300 square miles. "From the ranch house, it is two hours on a rough road to reach this place," he says. "We come to relax—to fish with the children and enjoy the hot springs."

The only other party we encounter in nearly two weeks consists of two young men named Jared Jellison and Robert Carpenter, and they are standing in canoes amid bags of gear and paddling hard upstream. The pair have been doing this for hundreds of miles from the Rio Grande's mouth, and they intend to keep going against the current until they run out of water. Over a shared dinner, we discover that they actually started on the lower Missouri in May of the previous year and have been going up or down linked rivers ever since, occasionally portaging over divides. The plan is to eventually log 30,000 continuous river miles, which they hope will stand as a new record.

"The longest trip I'd done before this was down the Osage River for 60 miles," Jellison tells me. Basically, he explains, they are a couple of guys who were doing construction work in Kansas City when they looked at each other one day and said: This sucks, let's go paddle.

I'd wager that many a renowned mountain man and explorer in America started with pretty much the same rationale. When I press Carpenter for more of the reason behind this adventure, he sweeps an arm toward the Rio Grande glimmering under the stars and says, "You don't really need a reason to spend time on a river, do you?"

Two members of our party have come from England to spend time on the Big River of the North. One, Hilary Speller, is an investment advisor. The second, Geoffrey Boyfield, age 69, worked as an electronics engineer and telecommunications systems analyst. "My knees wore out, so rafting is a good way left for me to enjoy the outdoors," he says simply. Boyfield has rarely been quite so far outdoors for so long. "The remoteness is quite wonderful," he tells me. "There is nothing but uninhabited country for miles and miles, and the isolation puts you in an entirely new frame of mind."

One morning, I catch up with the rafts to find Boyfield paddling in the front of a two-person kayak that the guides brought along. "The only other time I ever paddled a boat was on a river in Belgium," he calls across the water to me, "and I believe there was another boat a meter

Commonly thought of as another curious, spiky form of cactus, ocotillo actually belongs to a separate family of desert specialists more closely related to primroses and olives. Silhouetted against a sunset, it invokes its alternate name: coachwhip.

As guide Ursula Schmitt, a Blackfeet Indian, soaks away the river's mud and desert dust in the clear, warm springs next to Hot Springs Rapids, time itself seems to dissolve. It becomes easy to imagine a similar scene 9,000 years earlier, when the first Native Americans took up residence in the Rio Grande region, drawn by the rich plant and animal life flourishing along the river corridor.

away in every direction." That night by the fire, he muses, "There is so much natural beauty and peacefulness to be had in a place like this, it really makes you wonder what we've done to the rest of the world."

Toward the latter part of the trip, it is almost as if the rest of the world no longer even existed except as stories we recall. Most everyone is quieter than in the early days. Perhaps from being constantly overlooked by so many eons of Earth's history layered in the cliff walls, we all have a sense of being somewhat smaller in the scheme of things than we liked to think, somewhat more fleeting and vulnerable. At the same time, the group is knitting together, as parties sharing splendors, hardships, and daily routines in the backcountry will. My impression is reinforced nightly around the flickering campfire (built on a metal plate to keep from leaving a mark): We may be just a bunch of electronic-age folk with the luxury of indulging in a temporary river getaway, but we're still taking on aspects of a tribe.

I will be sorry to see the People of the Raft Clan disperse. But eventually, after a spell of relentless headwinds, with the guides working the raft oars like rowers on a slave galley, and a collision with a mid-rapids rock that catapults one client into the drink, we reach the pullout spot and prepare to go our separate ways.

In 1962, three million cubic meters of water flowed from the Rio Grande's mouth into the Gulf of Mexico. From 1990 through 1995, the average annual outflow was... zero. In other words, after being restored by the Rio Conchos, the Big River gets the life sucked out of it all over again.

Where and when this river does flow, recharged by winter snowmelt or rains, officials fear the contaminant load from croplands and urban areas may be causing health problems in people living along the banks, particularly on the Mexican side. The human population of the 180,000-square mile Rio Grande Basin is presently more than 15 million and increasing at a dramatic rate, especially along the Texas-Mexico border—that is, along the river itself. We have a lot more to do than declare two lengths of its flow wild and scenic. On the other hand, those two are an invaluable foundation on which to begin rebuilding a vital waterway.

At our farewell dinner Ian Kean told me about Canada's Heritage

Rivers program. Composed of 28 free-flowing waterways so far, it is a less stringent version of the national WSR system in the U.S. His River League's goal is to strengthen protection for waterways north of the 49th parallel, many of which are little known by the public. The Hulahula, which Kean floats down Alaska's North Slope, would be a good example, or the powerful, salmon-rich, mine-threatened Taku, running from First Nations (Native American) territory in northern British Columbia through the coastal range to emerge near Juneau, Alaska.

"Rivers are the ultimate metaphor for life," he observed. "In their wake, they provide nourishment for forests, wildlife, and people. They have always been conduits for human travel and migration, and I think that no matter how modern we are, a river trip reawakens old, deep connections. Without healthy rivers, we are lost."

I don't ever want to write: Go see the Rio Grande in its magnificent canyons while it still flows. Far better to say: Whoever is fortunate enough to float a WSR like the Rio Grande is likely to come away with a new commitment to keeping rivers and the life they sustain healthy together.

Riders on the first raft through San Francisco Rapids watch other boaters on the River League expedition work their way through the rocky shallows, trying to avoid the undercut cliff face directly below.

Perhaps only the moon has been around long enough to appreciate the eons

of Earth's history represented by these layers of rock that enfold the Rio Grande.

RECREATIONAL: Newfound Freedom for the Sudbury, Assabet, & Concord

After pausing to rest and refuel along a Massachusetts river, this migrating shorebird

Photographs by Brian Peterson

carries the flow of wildness on between its tundra nesting grounds and its southern wintering site.

*"...But I go with my friend
to the shore of our little river, and with one
stroke of the paddle I leave the village politics
and personalities....and pass into a delicate
realm of sunset and moonlight...."*

—RALPH WALDO EMERSON

ON THE HIGHWAY between Concord and West Concord in eastern Massachusetts, a local speed-limit sign comes with the advisory: Thickly Settled. Concord was founded as an extension of the Massachusetts Bay colony in 1635. Settlement has been thickening ever since. Heavy traffic rolls between colonial-era homes and shops, old brick factory buildings that now house Internet companies, and metropolitan Boston, with its population of several million, some 20 miles east.

But where a bridge takes the road over the Sudbury River, a weathered wooden boathouse hugs one bank, and a gangway runs from the deck down to a broad dock. Lined up all along its length are canoes. My reflex is automatic: I pull off the asphalt and rent one. Within minutes, I am paddling an avenue of calm—of liquid murmurings where painted turtles sun themselves amid reflections of silver maples and soft September clouds.

Three-quarters of a mile downstream, the canoe is practically in urban Concord. Yet forest and pasture still line much of the shores. Willow brush wades on out a few feet, offering perches for belted kingfishers and green herons. At Egg Rock, not far from the town

Kayaker Tony Laughrey (opposite) glides into a new day on the Sudbury River. The Sudbury, Assabet, and Concord were the first waterways designated partly for their literary values, recognizing the many writers the area nurtured. One, Henry David Thoreau, greeted dawn at Walden Pond (above), where he discovered transcendent beauty in natural settings, including the smallest, leafy details.

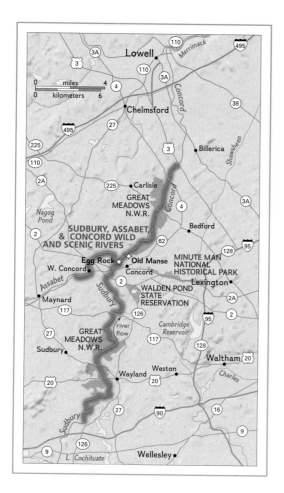

The Concord River forms as the Sudbury and Assabet merge. In 1999, all three became part of the National Wild and Scenic Rivers system. Although some of the protected river miles pass through Great Meadows National Wildlife Refuge, most adjoin private lands in a densely populated part of Massachusetts rich in history.

center, the Sudbury joins the Assabet River, arriving from the southwest. They form the Concord River, which continues northward but so gently that golden leaves freshly fallen on its surface are easily pushed upstream by a breeze.

Not far from its origin, the Concord's 100-foot width is spanned by an arched footbridge. Pulling in to the western bank, I pause to watch whirligig beetles dancing on the river's transparent skin. Then I climb a few steps past some mallard ducks to find a monument inscribed with the words:

> *By the rude bridge that arched the flood*
> *Their flag to April's breeze unfurled*
> *Here once the embattled farmers stood*
> *And fired the shot heard round the world.*

On April 19, 1775, colonial militia gathered on one side of the channel, and British redcoats sent to seize reported stockpiles of arms and munitions formed ranks on the other. The exchange of gunfire

that followed ignited the American Revolution. Now, handfuls of visitors stroll a gravel path between small, informative plaques. Deer tracks pattern the mud here and there. The Old North Bridge section of Minute Man National Historical Park feels as tranquil as it is unpretentious. Only the cardinal flowers on the shaded bank, their scarlet hue designed to attract hummingbird pollinators, invoke a sense of the blood once spilled in pursuit of liberty.

Much of the peaceful atmosphere seeps across from the property next door. Known as the Old Manse, it is a carefully restored colonial home and grounds owned by the Trustees of Reservations, a private group that works closely with the National Park Service to maintain the original setting. This was the family home of Ralph Waldo Emerson, who penned those lines about the shot heard round the world.

Poet, essayist, minister, and leading early 19th-century intellectual, Emerson wrote: "My house stands in low land, with limited outlook, and on the skirt of a village. But I go with my friend to the

On an April day 224 years before the Concord River was designated wild and scenic, colonial minutemen assembled on one side of the old North Bridge and British redcoats on the other. The musket fire that rang out over the quiet waters heralded the American Revolution.

While a couple head upstream from a boat rental shop on the Sudbury, other canoes await their moment in the sun. Many will

carry paddlers from the Boston metropolitan area 20 miles east, letting urbanites slip loose from a hectic, high-rise existence.

shore of our little river, and with one stroke of the paddle I leave the village politics and personalities....and pass into a delicate realm of sunset and moonlight...."

He and his Concord environs became the focal point for a group of New Englanders involved in a distinctly American movement. It was called transcendentalism, the goal being to transcend our usual perceptions of the materialistic world and become more conscious of the spirit that pervades all things. Man and nature are part of a divine unity, adherents said, and you don't have to rely on religious scholars or musty Old World texts to interpret it. Take a walk. Go for a paddle. Open yourself directly to the beauty and fullness of creation.

While living at the Old Manse, Emerson completed the essay "Nature," his exposition of transcendentalism's ideals. Then, in 1840, he helped found *The Dial,* a magazine that published like-minded authors such as Ellery Channing, Bronson Alcott (whose daughter Louisa May Alcott won fame for the book *Little Women*), and Elizabeth Peabody. Their philosophy called for a break from traditional notions of humans as inherently sinful and nature as an adversary to be subjugated. They also questioned a social order that disenfranchised not only Native Americans and black Americans but half of its Caucasian citizenry because of its sex.

"We would have every path laid open to Woman as freely as to Man...," proclaimed Margaret Fuller, editor of *The Dial* and a pioneer of the feminist movement. "As the friend of the negro assumes that one man cannot, by right, hold another in bondage, so should the friend of Woman assume that Man cannot, by right, lay even well-meant restrictions on Woman." In a sense, these Concord reformers carried on the battle for independence begun at the neighboring bridge.

When the future author of *The Scarlet Letter*, Nathaniel Hawthorne, arrived with his new bride, Sophia Peabody, to begin a three-year stay at Old Manse, a local named Henry planted the garden as a wedding gift and taught Hawthorne how to row. Given to wading in the Assabet wearing nothing but a hat, wandering on long walks through the woods, and, most famously, living alone for two years on land Emerson owned by the shore of nearby Walden Pond, Henry David Thoreau didn't just hear a different drummer, but also coined the phrase.

Described as everything from a literary giant to the prototype for hippies, this fellow was wary of enterprises that required new clothes, wary even of the rustic business of farming, feeling that it, too, chained people to production. Though a skilled craftsman and professional surveyor himself, Thoreau couldn't have agreed less with his busy, young country's assumption that the key to the good life lay in ever expanding commerce and industry.

"Absolutely speaking," he said, "the more money, the less virtue." In *Walden*, he wrote, "But lo! men have become the tools of their tools," and, "Most of the stone a nation hammers goes toward its tomb only. It buries itself alive." For all their admiration of nature, most transcendentalists tended to view the out-of-doors as a backdrop to the human quest for a grand moral vision. Thoreau celebrated the wild realm more for its own sake. In its vastness on this continent, in its beckoning grandeurs and freedoms, he sensed what made the New World truly new.

Concord's writers and thinkers are one of

On Walden Pond acreage owned by a friend, the poet and philosopher Ralph Waldo Emerson, Thoreau built a small but comfortable cabin with his own hands. Striving for self-sufficiency, he took pride in completing the task for exactly 28 dollars, twelve-and-a-half cents.

Indians knew the Sudbury as Musketaquid, meaning grass-river, here

seen meandering through Great Meadows National Wildlife Refuge.

Much like paddlers converging in a channel, people from eight different towns and many walks of life came together to win protection for the Sudbury, Assabet, and Concord and to develop a plan that gives local communities a major role in managing these national wild and scenic rivers.

the main reasons behind something else truly new: In 1999, the Sudbury, Assabet, and Concord Rivers joined the WSR system. Of the miles included, 14.9 are classified as scenic, 14.1 as recreational, and all 29 count as the first ever placed under management to "protect and enhance...literary resources" along with other values. The idea is to honor the area's artistic heritage, especially given its influence on America's environmental consciousness. Had Thoreau, Emerson, and their colleagues never scribbled a word, we might not be doing things like protecting rivers and wildlands today.

Among the many who worked for years to save these three waterways is Betsy Stokey, who grew up in the area. A social services counselor, often dealing with difficult child custody cases, she is also the volunteer president of OAR, the Organization for the Assabet River. On a sunlit fall morning, we off-load a canoe from her car top

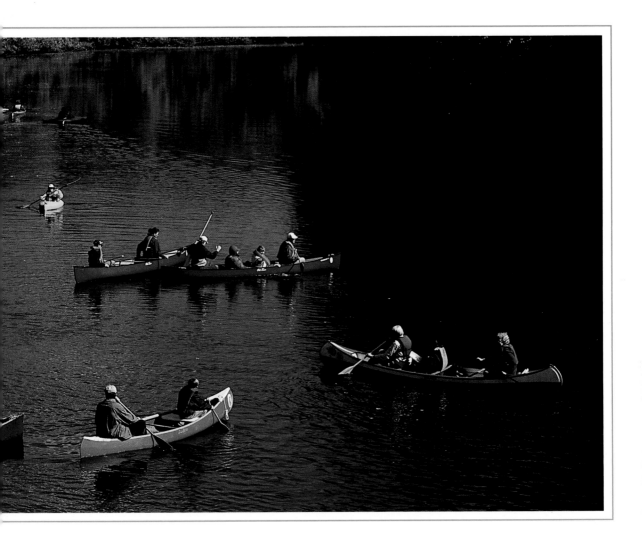

just below the dam that once fed Damon Mill, a wool factory, and ease through the duckweed of a old sluiceway into the current.

Some of the maples are beginning to flame at their tips with autumn colors. One giant has toppled across the channel. As we carry the canoe around, Stokey asks, "Can you smell the wild grapes?" In a moment, I'm snacking on a handful. People call them fox grapes. "A local man managed to blend their hardiness with the taste of domestic grapes." His name was Ephraim Bull, and his invention, the Concord grape, became America's first commercially cultivated table variety.

A mink's prints along the shore lead to the remains of its food, a mound of crayfish skeletons. Great blue herons stalk the shallows trying to spear fish. Nipmuck Indians who lived here probably did the same—when not munching grapes. I can make out perch and bull-heads everywhere, not because the Assabet has more fish than the other rivers, but because it offers better visibility. Narrowest and swiftest of the river trio, it has cut its way down to bedrock interspersed with beds of light, mica-flecked granite sand.

Confined by high banks, the rushing Assabet quickly became the favorite of dam-builders and industries. While Hawthorne, in *Mosses from an Old Manse*, enthused, "A more lovely stream than this, for a mile above its junction with the Concord, has never flowed on earth...," Thoreau was lamenting, "So completely emasculated and demoralized is our river that it is even made to observe the Christian Sabbath," referring to the fact that the flow was lowest on Sundays, when the gates of upstream impoundments were closed. The water was already loaded with effluents in his time, and for decades thereafter, people commented about the river running red one day and Union blue the next, according to which dyes the textile factories were using.

A high percentage of the Assabet's present flow is withdrawn by neighboring towns, farms, and industries (much of this from wells in the Assabet watershed) and then returned somewhat soiled. During dry months, as much as 80 percent of the river's volume may consist of discharge from the seven different wastewater treatment plants along its length. Their outflow is less toxic than it was in the 1970s, before regulations forced the removal of heavy metals. But levels of phospho-

Concord means agreement. A harmony of interests. Balance. Peace. In perfect concord with the river's smooth skin, Sylvia Willard, from the nearby town of Carlisle, sculls along like a giant water strider.

rus, which fertilizes excessive algae growth, are still far too high, and so are summer counts of coliform bacteria, an indicator of excrement. There is also more non-point source pollution—the runoff of silt and chemicals from lawns, pavement, and other surfaces—all the time.

Despite such insults, the Assabet's lower four miles, making up the WSR section, offer some of the area's loveliest, most remote-feeling tableaus. Around a slender bend, ferns line the channel while interlacings of pine, hemlock, maple, and oak completely overarch it. Mourning doves call from the green shade and flutter down to sip at the water's edge. Dozens of painted turtles huddle in the sunny spots that manage to penetrate the bower. According to Stokey, we have a chance of seeing snapping turtles, although Blandings turtles and spotted turtles have become rare.

I am aware of rooftops now and then and of an occasional barking dog or lawn mower above the sound of riffles. At other times, civilization might have withdrawn to Boston for all I can tell. River magic is strong stuff for warding off the world's hurly-burly, but these three rivers have had help. The towns have a long tradition of acquiring land for open space, sometimes leasing it back to farmers to preserve agriculture. In 1953, a foresighted and gifted community organizer named Allen Morgan formed the Sudbury Valley Trustees. His group began safeguarding riverside lands through conservation easements and purchases. Momentum built as the Nature Conservancy, Trust for Public Land, and other private associations joined in.

The Clean Water Act of 1965 began to seriously reverse the centuries-long slide in water quality. Next came Massachusetts Wetlands Protection Act in the 1970s, followed in the 1990s by the state's Rivers Protection Act. With few exceptions, it prohibits the building of new structures within 200 feet of shorelines. Additional laws governing wetlands and floodplains reinforce those restrictions, as does the fairly strict local zoning applied within this historic locale.

Drifting over a stretch of sand so bright that I can follow fish shadows brings a smile of recognition. I was wading here just yesterday with a big plastic bag over my shoulder and rubber gloves on my hands. It was OAR's 14th annual river cleanup. Up and down the channel, others slogged along hauling everything from discarded tires

Autumn air injects the colors of fire into waterscapes, especially where maple branches arc out from the banks. Given the number of writers and other artists produced along the shores of the Concord and its tributaries, it seems that some of nature's inventiveness rubbed off directly onto the human populace.

You don't need a kayak to negotiate the Assabet, swiftest and rockiest of the three wild and scenic waterways, but it makes a fine way to dart from riffle to reflecting pool.

to baby buggies. If a culture is revealed by the makeup of its garbage, our main discovery was rather predictable: folks around these parts really like beer. A few oddly shaped bottles emptied by their great-grandparents turned up as well.

At intervals, I toted my mucky bounty up to a collection point run by Dave Partington. "I work with my hands, avoid 9-to-5 jobs, and volunteer a lot"—a bit of the Thoreau philosophy—the craftsman and sometimes carpenter told me. "When I was a child, my father had me pick up other people's trash on the street. I guess you could say I was taught early that the Earth is not self-cleaning."

Dumping a load beside me, Jeremy Adams, who recently moved to the area and does desktop publishing, shrugged and said, "Simple: I like to kayak the river. It's full of crap, and I want to help get it out. Also, my girlfriend doesn't like to kayak as much as I do. I figure if it looks nicer, she might be more willing to come."

Mike Farny, who used to do water-quality planning for the joint state-federal New England River Basin Commission, added, "I couldn't see the bottom of the Assabet 32 years ago. There was filamentous algae from bank to bank, rainbows of petroleum, and clusters of dead fish at the base of dams. So we've come a long way, but we have far to go. We really have no choice but to clean up our own home."

"It's all our backyards," Stokey is musing now while we drift

onward, passing over a native mussel bed. Because freshwater mussels reflect the condition of rivers, the fact that they may be the most imperiled group of animals in America ought to serve as a wake-up call. New England has 12 of the 297 remaining U.S. species. Seven in Massachusetts are listed as endangered or "of special concern." Looking over the shells half-buried in clean sand below, I think: maybe lugging beer bottles and rotted sneakers out of the Assabet is more symbolic than truly useful. Trash is among the least of the threats to its wild inhabitants. But then again, every step in the right direction, however small, adds up. I mean, a guy could bring his girlfriend kayaking over a spot like this. And who knows? She might be inspired to fight for stronger pollution controls or write a book that would eclipse the finest transcendentalist passages.

It wasn't water power that first drew the attention of settlers but the great floodplain meadows along the slower, more meandering rivers. They promised a bounty of livestock fodder. The marshes are broadest along the Sudbury, which, along with the Concord, the Indians called Musketaquid, or grass-river. I paddle up it one evening with Julia Blatt, the executive director of OAR.

Good-size fish cause sudden boils on the surface where they snatch food, but I can't see well enough through the silty, brown water to tell whether they are bass or carp. The banks, pocked with muskrat

Pedal power carries travelers along the Assabet to its confluence with the Sudbury. A variety of trails are scattered throughout the area. With support from the National Park Service's Rivers and Trails Conservation Assistance program, locals hope to link them together, creating a continuous system of hiking and biking paths in the half-mile-wide protected corridors of the three wild and scenic rivers.

burrows, are mostly black mud brightened at intervals by the violet flower spikes of pickerelweed or orange jewelweed blossoms. Beyond, cattails and reeds seem to stretch away forever beneath a sunset sky full of cloud flare and tinted bird wings.

We are winding through Great Meadows National Wildlife Refuge, established in 1944 to protect these wetlands. The original refuge consisted of 250 donated acres, including what is now a separate unit just north of Minute Man National Historical Park on the Concord River. Later land donations and occasional purchases have brought the total to more than 3,600 acres.

About 12 of the river trio's 29 WSR miles adjoin refuge property. They make a nice fit, both ecologically and in terms of more recent literary heritage. William Brewster, who taught at Harvard and lived near the Old Manse, produced detailed accounts of the region's natural history from 1886 through 1917. His successor, Ludlow Griscom, published noted works in ornithology such as *Birds of Concord* and

Generations of discards have found their way into the Assabet River as it runs through Massachusetts towns. Each year, volunteers participating in a cleanup day bring a few more tons back up onto the shore for proper disposal, leaving the bottom a little brighter for the resident freshwater mussels, turtles, and fish and for boaters drifting above.

encouraged later generations of keen-eyed observers. Each year now, the refuge hosts more than 220 bird species and 350,000 people, mostly avid bird-watchers.

At the base of a low hill, deer graze among silhouettes of swamp oaks in the deepening dusk. Northern harriers—marsh hawks—come gliding above the cattails. With primordial smells saturating the air and prehuman voices welcoming the first stars, I am again amazed that such timeless moods persist in a place so long and so thickly settled.

Blatt and her many partners in the Rivers Stewardship Council and the SuAsCo Watershed Coalition are more aware of other things in the watery mix. Mercury. Arsenic. Lead. PCBs. Name a poison. Signs warn people not to eat the fish. What are the herons, minks, and occasional otters supposed to do? What of the fish themselves? An industrial complex called Nyanza, a Superfund site, leaks mercury and other contaminants into the upper Sudbury. Along the Assabet, where earlier factories produced gunpowder, a company made armor-piercing bullets tipped with spent uranium and dumped an estimated million-plus pounds of radioactive and toxic wastes into unlined pits. The brew has leached down into groundwater migrating toward the river. It's a special concern if you get thirsty downstream in Billerica, which still takes its drinking water from the Concord.

"Then we have less dramatic issues like the proliferation of large, emerald-green lawns and golf courses," Blatt says. "The tremendous amount of water required to keep these lawns green during dry weather depletes both the groundwater and the surface water in the watershed, and the fertilizers people put on the lawns runs off into the nearest storm drains, eventually ending up in the river. We end up with a green, fertilized river—not a pretty sight for fish or people. We'll declare success when kids can safely go swimming again and the fish are fit to eat."

As a sign of optimism, the SuAsCo coalition is working with federal and state fisheries managers to reintroduce shad, a large, tasty herring that in Emerson's time annually migrated from the Atlantic into these waterways to spawn. The first step involves reestablishing smaller fish called alewives, a favorite shad food. Pam Hess, a public information officer for Great Meadows refuge, tells me, "Our area sees the odd black bear and fisher, and the Nashua River has moose and

Moveable feast:
Outings along the
Sudbury and Concord
include regular evening
pontoon boat dinner
cruises and the occasional
special catered affair.

bobcats. That's only 20 miles away." In other words, the rivers' ecosystem could become a little wilder and more scenic.

On one of many floats down the Concord, I beach at the refuge's Concord Unit to hike its trails. The marsh has been temporarily drained. Managers do this to reduce exotic plant invaders, increase native vegetation, and expose mudflats to feed migrating shorebirds. In the meantime, waddling blankets of Canada geese take advantage of newly exposed plant shoots, while herons and egrets plunder the fish in drying pools.

One of the larger pools holds figures that are either swamp monsters or two of the dirtiest humans on the East Coast. Eventually, I recognize Stephanie Kosh, a refuge biologist, and Lisa Plagge, a biological technician, stumbling through the ooze among hundreds of huge, stranded carp. These fish are also unwanted exotics, but the more pressing reason to remove them is that if too many die in a stagnant pool, their decay can trigger an outbreak of avian botulism. After watching the women get splattered with yet another mud layer each time they net a writhing carp, I leave, certain that if this aquatic system is never put back into balance, it won't be for lack of trying.

Apart from the refuge and Minute Man park, the shoreline property is controlled by hundreds of individual owners and eight different townships. As Pam Hess puts it, "If you want to get something accomplished here, you have no choice but to work with your neighbors." The effort to win WSR status for the three rivers lasted well over a decade.

Bill Sullivan, a real estate developer, served on Concord's Board of Selectmen (city council) and subsequently as chairman of the Wild and Scenic River Study Committee for the three rivers. When we meet at the old Damon Mill, which he restored as a six-story office building, he tells me, "I think a lot of the preservation instinct here comes from the fact that we still maintain an open town-meeting system. It's direct representation and supports more of a sense of community. The threat of 'takings' of private property became an issue because the Wild and Scenic Rivers Act gives the government the right to take up to 1,500 feet on either side of a river. In this part of the world, where land can be worth more than a million dollars an acre, that's a big deal."

The final WSR legislation ensured that all eight shoreline

communities were part of the Sudbury, Assabet, and Concord Rivers Stewardship Council set up to guide management. In addition, the WSR agreement included a special clause guaranteeing that there would be no federal "takings." These two provisions added up to an unprecedented emphasis on local control.

What exactly does WSR protection do for the river complex, then? I ask Jamie Fosburgh, who oversees WSR management in the New York-New England area for the National Park Service, the lead federal agency. Guiding me through the woods to the base of one of the 22 bridges that span the river trio, he says, "The Massachusetts Department of Highways plans to turn the four-lane road into a six-lane and replace this double-arch bridge. They need federal dollars to do it. That triggers a review by us, which means we have a chance to talk about historic qualities, scenic values, what sort of redesign would improve wildlife corridors, and so forth. Engineers are looking at the bridge from the standpoint of cost-efficiency. We try to do it from the standpoint of a canoeist or a deer. We have to be reasonable, but nothing gets built until we sign off on the permit."

The same authority can be extended to federally funded activities miles away in the watershed if they involve water resources projects

Straining for speed atop a placid flow, the rowing team from Middlesex School, a college preparatory academy on the Concord's shore, practices its strokes.

"One day the sun shall shine...into our minds and hearts, and light up our whole lives with a

great awakening light, as warm and serene and golden as a bankside in autumn." —Henry David Thoreau

that would harm the wild and scenic rivers. And although land condemnation is prohibited, WSRA standards encourage careful riverside planning. Since the act authorizes the Park Service to work with communities through the Rivers and Trails Conservation Assistance program, supporters may realize their dream of completing pathways along the Concord and Assabet sooner than expected. Finally, the WSRA can direct some federal money to private groups that arrange conservation easements on riverine lands.

"Of all the rivers in our system, this is the most developed, and it flows through the most densely populated area." Fosburgh adds. "In a way, the SuAsCo is our model for working with communities." Another river he works on, the Lamprey, in New Hampshire, is almost completely within private holdings, and yet it recently won wild and scenic river designation too.

As the Concord nears Billerica, it grows steadily wider, looking less like an intimate village stream and more like something you could sail on, a pleasure Thoreau described in *A Week on the Concord and Merrimack*

Rivers. Two other protected waterways in the northeast quadrant of the nation are downright huge. One is northwestern Pennsylvania's Allegheny, with 85 WSR miles. The other, the Delaware, running between Pennsylvania, New York, and New Jersey, has 175.7 WSR miles, 35 of them in the Delaware Water Gap National Recreation Area. Though within half a day's drive of at least 50 million people, this remains one of the biggest free-flowing U.S. rivers outside Alaska.

Private lands embrace 93 percent of the Delaware and the great majority of the Allegheny as well—further evidence that you don't have to keep looking in the more remote parts of America to find wild and scenic rivers. They are where you make them. Yes, this national system is invaluable in preserving a healthy environment. But perhaps the ultimate natural resource it showcases will be people's ability to work side by side for the good of the whole. The Sudbury, Assabet, and Concord trio is a shining example. Concord, after all, means harmony, consensus. And what have rivers always done if not naturally draw people together and carry them along a common course?

Where Thoreau sought solitude at Walden Pond, some 600,000 people now arrive every year. Many visit to learn more about early America's famed spokesman for the spiritual values of wildness. But the majority simply come to picnic and play. Set aside as a state reserve, the lake and its surroundings remain relatively pristine, and unpolluted swimming water is an all-too-rare treasure in the greater Boston area.

Sun-gilded pond lilies are a reminder of what writers past and present keep

telling us: True riches are free, and nature provides them in infinite supply.

Reflections on the Course Ahead

YELLOWSTONE RIVER Almost every river in the greater Yellowstone ecosystem is

wild and scenic, though only Clarks Fork in Wyoming has been officially designated as such.

*"We've got to make people understand
the importance of habitat linkages to
animal movements and genetics,
and we've got to do it in a hurry or
we're pretty much going to run out
of possibilities."*
—BUZZ WILLIAMS

HARLEQUIN DUCKS are white-water fanatics, fine-feathered kayakers inclined toward the extreme. They winter among the breakers that pound rocky Pacific shores, then fly inland to breed along swift mountain flows. They like their rivers far from disturbance, and they like them tousled by rapids. In a patchwork plumage of cinnamon and blue with white and black markings, these birds foot-paddle through cascades, dive amid uproars of waves, and pop back to the swirling surface bearing stone fly nymphs in their mouths, as if to say, "What was the big deal about that Class IV stretch?" Some of them summer so high in the headwaters that mountain goats watch their maneuvers.

Wherever harlequins are present, wildness is the rule rather than the exception. They are an indicator of the most intact watersheds in the Pacific Northwest and points north. On a trip through Montana's Bob Marshall Wilderness Area and Great Bear Wilderness to survey harlequins with a team of biologists, I crossed grizzly tracks on the sandbars and heard a wolf howl above the night whispers of the stream flowing by camp.

COLORADO RIVER

The Colorado's handiwork includes Arizona's mile-deep Grand Canyon (opposite) and slopes that passing rains can suddenly leave deep in wildflowers (above). Dam proposals that would have flooded this scenic wonder were among the threats that sparked passage of the National Wild and Scenic Rivers Act. Ironically, the famed Colorado itself has not yet been designated.

We traveled by horseback up and over the Continental Divide from the east, wading mile after sunlit mile of clear, trouty streambeds. Partway down the western slope, I unsaddled and jumped with my backpack into a two-man kayak with researcher David Lee. We pushed off into the Middle Fork of the Flathead, a wild and scenic river that continues through the wilderness to eventually become the southern boundary of Glacier National Park.

In places, the mountainsides closed in as purple-red walls. The boat lay suspended between them on deep, luminous pools with secondary pools of great silence overhead. A hundred yards later, the Middle Fork would start down a steep gradient littered with boulders and transform us from soft-spoken, contemplative types into joyriders yee-hawing around in a big outdoor washing machine. Our overloaded little rubber craft spilled so often that we came out clean as tumbled river stones.

THE THREE FORKS OF THE FLATHEAD RIVER—North, Middle, and South—are the lifeblood of one of the most robust wildlife communities left in the lower 48 states. Here is a Rocky Mountain ensemble with nearly all the original players, from bighorn sheep, lynx, and wolverines to bull trout and westslope cutthroats. It is headlined by the densest grizzly population in the U.S. outside Alaska. Brothers John and Frank Craighead, known for their groundbreaking studies of the great bears, became leading advocates for the protection of Flathead waters after a dam drowned the lower South Fork and plans for another, on the Middle Fork, seemed about to be set in concrete.

As noted in Chapter One of this book, the Craigheads were instrumental in bringing about the 1968 Wild and Scenic Rivers Act (WSRA). In 1976, they helped add the North, Middle, and upper South Forks of the Flathead to the system. People across the nation owe the naturalist twins a debt of gratitude for their vision. I owe more than most, and not only for good journeys on many an untamed waterway. My wife and I have a home in the remote bottomlands of the Flathead's North Fork. Although we aren't there full-time these days, we were for 11 years until our children reached school age. This wild and scenic river outlines Glacier Park's western edge, the eastern boundary of our property, and a good portion of our lives.

*D*URING THE WARM MONTHS, we awake to the sound of water falling over a beaver dam on a creek leading to the river channel. Then, while the sun climbs across the Great Divide in Glacier, we wander down to the channel to splash our faces and see which of the neighbors are up and about. They might be goldeneye ducks, mergansers, belted kingfishers, bald eagles, perhaps a moose among the beaver-gnawed willows, a patrolling mink—the possibilities seem unending, for the riverway is the busiest part of the ecosystem.

Black bears and grizzlies are usually around. In early summer, the big silver-tipped bears move to cottonwood groves on the river's gravel bars and dig up the starchy roots of a wild vetch until acres lie pocked with craters and freshly overturned soil. More grizz show up during autumn as the hawthorne and the serviceberries and other fruits ripen along incoming streams.

Through the six long months of winter, the floodplains of the river are bustling and are more important than ever to the region's deer, elk, and moose. They find food in the form of riverside shrubs, and the traveling is easy compared to higher elevations, where snows pile up shoulder deep. The bottomlands' spruce, cottonwoods, and firs, giant old-timers whose branches intercept the snowfall like roofs, always offer a few pockets of completely bare ground along with shelter from fierce winds and sub-zero skies. As key winter range for hoofed wildlife, the valley floor becomes equally important to coyotes, cougars, and a species absent from the West for half a century—wolves, which came from Canada and settled in not long after we did.

My wife and I are at our North Fork home right now. While dishes prepared for a Thanksgiving dinner warm atop the woodstove back in the cabin, we work up an appetite skating with friends along a channel. The beavers have raised the height of their dam here with fresh cottonwood cuttings, giving us a long upstream expanse to glide upon. *(Continued on page 166)*

TAKU RIVER *A rafting group heads back toward Juneau on Alaska's rainy coast via the Taku, which arises*

in British Columbia and drains one of the largest unprotected wilderness watersheds on the continent's Pacific side.

TAKU RIVER

"Whose habitat?" a wandering black bear (above) seems to ask. Both black and grizzly bears rely on the Taku's tremendous salmon runs, as do Tlingit Indians in British Columbia and Alaskan commercial fishermen. A Canadian company's plans to greatly expand an old mine site (right) on a tributary, the Tulsequah, and build a 100-mile service road from the coast could suddenly inject high levels of pollution and human disturbance into the remote wildland expanse.

TAKU RIVER Voyagers gazing up at raw crags and avalanche slopes might

assume that the real mother lode to be found along the Taku is its unspoiled grandeur.

(Continued from page 159) A skift of snow covers the ice, and the fine crystals preserve even the delicate tracks of deer mice. Cruising on our blades over the crisscrossings of paw prints and the occasional impression of wings is like speed-reading a story. Halfway along, an eruption of broad, sideways strokes obliterates the calligraphy of small animal sign. We follow the odd smears to the shore. They turn into deep holes in the snowpack—elk tracks, far apart. Whether spooked or eager, the animal was moving in a hurry when it hit the ice and abruptly found all four hoofs sliding out from underneath its body in separate directions. It looks like 800 pounds of splayfooted elk went through a terrific comic routine before finally winning the battle with gravity. The record is from a colder day, for where the performer exited, the ice has become a crescent of open water with an ouzel bobbing in it, hunting insect larvae among the rounded river rocks.

The bird gives off a bright series of notes, and they bring to mind other days when my wife and I followed wolf or elk tracks on the river. I remember following the fish under its glassy new ice too, cross-country skating on it all the way to the Canadian border, and playing hockey next to the slide marks of an otter family. After the melt got underway, we bathed in the current and shouted out its cold. We explored its algae, insects, and frogs with the children; hauled garden water from it; snorkeled in it; and rode it with canoes, rafts, inner tubes, and an old surfboard, not to mention a shark, killer whale, and alligator—the kids' inflatable toys. Finally, we simply sat by it for untold hours. We came to know this river's lights and moods and assemblage of lives as well as we knew anything in the world. They became part of me, and I still carry them wherever I go.

So THIS IS NOT A BOOK about wild and scenic rivers by an unbiased reporter. I am a grateful beneficiary of this national system that Americans invented. Although plans to dam the North Fork were put forward in the 1940s and lingered for the next couple of decades, I don't have to worry about them appearing again in response to the latest energy crunch, and none of the wild neighbors does either. Over the years, WSR status has helped deflect schemes for strip-mining coal in the North Fork's Canadian headwaters and for replacing the winding dirt road on the U.S. side with a high-speed highway.

Funds made available through the WSRA allowed the lead management agency for the Flathead's three forks, the U.S. Forest Service, to buy riverside land from willing sellers. Other owners sold or donated conservation easements that restrict subdivision, waterfront commercial ventures, and related activities. We have such covenants on our place. The private parcel next to ours became national forest through a government trade with the owner. A mile north, the Forest Service purchased a privately owned strip where side channels braid through willow and dogwood brush. And so the process continued up and down the WSR corridor. The Nature Conservancy, Montana Land Reliance, and other nonprofit groups joined the effort to acquire acreage and easements, expanding the scope of protection across the floodplain and up onto the benchlands that overlook the river from the west.

Mind you, none of this has halted growth. The North Fork sees more homesites, residents, and modern impacts in the riverine environment every year. What WSR status has done is damp down the rate of growth while spurring discussion about how best to deal with further increases. People everywhere say they want to balance human expansion with the preservation of natural values they cherish. But development has a way of getting out ahead of our ability to shape it. The WSRA provides one means of catching up.

FOR ALL MY TIME WITH RIVERS, I still have far to go to understand them. Jack Stanford, director of the University of Montana's Flathead Lake Biological Station, has a knack for widening people's views, which is why I am traipsing behind him to the edge of the Middle Fork. The April water has turned from clear blue to spring green with the early melt at lower elevations. It will be late May or June before the snowpack gleaming far overhead among the peaks goes liquid. Once it does, this river will be brown and roiling with trees ripped from undercut banks, spilling across the valley in a *(Continued on page 174)*

COLUMBIA RIVER *Milliseconds from a meeting with the longest and*

mightiest river of the U.S. Pacific Northwest, swimmers begin a group plunge.

COLUMBIA RIVER *Despite 14 dams across its main stem and more than 250 across its tributaries, the Columbia*

still flows free along Hanford Reach, reserved for a nuclear facility and now proposed as a wild and scenic candidate.

KLICKITAT RIVER

Native American fisher-
men practice traditional
dipnetting for salmon on
a Columbia tributary,
Washington's Klickitat,
(upper left)—but with less
success every year. Along
with other factors, from
past overharvesting to
sedimentation from
logging, multiple dams
have reduced historical
runs of 16 million salmon
annually to mere thou-
sands. Sport fishermen
still enjoy whopping suc-
cess (lower middle) now
and then. But a lot of time
is spent looking (lower left
and lower right) at water
with no sign of salmon,
some of which used to
journey 1,100 miles up the
Columbia to spawn.

(Continued from page 167) round-the-clock roar. By July, it will be back in its present channel like a rebottled genie and so transparent you can count every cobble on its bottom.

*W*HATEVER LEVEL OF FLOW the Middle Fork presents, Stanford knows that he is looking at only part of the river. The rest is far beneath our shoes and hundreds or even thousands of feet to each side, running through heaps of glacial gravel that have filled the valley floor since the ice ages. Down in that sunless realm, water is caching sediments and organic debris among the stones, microbes are feeding and multiplying on it, and their colonies are fueling a subterranean aquatic food chain. Pointing to a large stone fly on my cap and a tiny one on my shirt collar, Stanford says, "We've found 42 species of stone flies among the insects living in the Middle Fork. Some pass their larval stages deep in the gravel, going about their lives 30 feet or more below what most people consider the bottom of the river."

Where I notice stunted cottonwood saplings near ranks of taller ones, he sees a sign that the invisible flow is down welling— sinking fast, depriving the roots of water during the hot months. What I had thought were leftover pools in a side channel, he knows to be spots where the hidden portion of the river wells up into view. The extra nitrogen it carries from the underground community accounts for the bright algae growth tinting the rocks. "The floodplain serves as a major storehouse for nutrients," Stanford explains. "It is also the warmest area around during winter and the coolest in summer." These conditions underpin the riverway's attraction for flora and fauna.

Stanford would go one step further and describe a river less as a place than as a process, a dynamic force that surges and ebbs, transports, buries, carves anew, and shifts course from side to side. Like avalanches and wildfires, a free-moving waterway is a major agent of change within forested mountain settings, continually creating new openings, early stages of plant succession, and opportunities for animals tied to those traditional habitats. Older habitats meanwhile benefit from fresh, fertile deposits of soil. Within the

Rockies, a river and its associated floodplain, wetlands, and riparian corridor amount to a pump that boosts the vitality of the ecosystem as a whole.

A similar pattern holds for unbridled rivers from coast to coast. Whatever the particular topography, they are the most productive and biologically diverse features within it, enriching the countryside for miles around. If you want to promote the health of the environment and ensure the survival of the greatest array of life-forms, protecting rivers is a good place to begin.

That is what the WSRA does. At its inception, the act was in good part a reactionary measure aimed at simply preventing dams and diversions from claiming waterways everywhere. It was a Keep Rivers Free movement made into law, and the priority was to save examples of the most pristine and spectacular flows. Since then, river protection, like other aspects of conservation, has broadened its focus. The goal is to sustain the integrity of ecosystems, not just in the wildest places but in every corner of the country. Given their average quarter-mile limit of influence on either shore, WSR corridors cannot accomplish that. But, as in the North Fork, they can kick start the task and provide a natural template for keeping habitats connected.

ONE OF THE VERY FIRST WSRs added to the system following passage of the WSRA, the Chattooga, and one of the latest to be designated, the Wekiva, make equally good examples. Although the Chattooga is not very wide or long, its watershed encompasses some 180,000 acres in three states in the Southern Appalachians. These are extremely old mountains, weathered into countless ridges and hollows or side valleys, each a world slightly apart from the rest. Never subject to ice age glaciers, this legacy of microniches goes hand in hand with a high level of biodiversity.

Appalachian waters hold an unparalleled assortment of freshwater mussels and crayfish and reflect a shoreline cane called arundinaria, linked to the life cycles of more than 20 species of moths and butterflies. The Cherokee Nation relied on this robust grass too, turning it into mats, baskets, and flutes. They cultivated butternut and walnut, two of the more than 130 tree species found in the Southern

GREEN RIVER

From snowy headwaters in west-central Wyoming, the Green roams a high, dry, lonesome chunk of the West before joining the Colorado River in southeastern Utah. With colorful gorges, explosive white-water sections, and peaceful meanderings in between, segments of the Green are often mentioned as possible additions to the national river system. Like many waterways in arid sagebrush country, the river is a magnet for plant and animal life and for recreation.

Appalachians, which contain half the known varieties of ferns and flowering plants on the continent. Among the soft leaf litter moldering below all those oaks, sycamores, basswoods, gums, hickories, maples, and rhododendrons dwell what may be the greatest array of salamanders on the globe.

You don't have to go very far along the Chattooga River to grasp how much more than the actual waterway the words wild and scenic describe. For that matter, you needn't even get into a boat. Instead, you can travel the Chattooga by foot or horseback on the more than 70 miles of trails through lands managed mainly by the Forest Service, which oversees the WSR. The choices include the Foothills National Recreation Trail and the Bartram Trail, named after William Bartram, who explored the Southeast and catalogued its natural history, carrying on the work of his father, John, often called the father of American botany.

I'M ON THE CHATTOOGA RIVER TRAIL, laid out mostly within the 15,704-acre WSR corridor yet often beyond sight of the main waterway. The river makes its presence known at a distance by sounds carried uphill on the wind or as a sudden ribbon of light glistening through the trees. I hardly ever feel that it is absent anyway, because the trail crosses a tributary at almost every bend. Sometimes it is a steep, strong freshet spanned by a bridge. More often, I hop over a small rill trickling among mossy rocks where amphibian eyes peer out from the damp recesses of a fern grotto like a miniature display of life many eons ago during Earth's Carboniferous period.

A few other hikers pass by—a golden-agers walking club, several families, and a couple of teenagers backpacking overnight gear—but I find plenty of solitude in between. Getting to know the Chattooga by stepping over its brooks brings home the fact that you can no more separate these woodlands from the river than a body from its circulatory system. But whereas the WSR corridor is managed for its natural values, the remainder of the national forest has been heavily managed for timber. Logging operations and the roads bulldozed to them slough off a good deal of sediment in a region soaked by around 80 inches of annual rainfall. More muddy runoff comes from the upper end of the watershed, where private lands are rapidly being subdivided.

Buzz Williams, a South Carolina native, worked as a river guide and Forest Service employee before helping found a watershed protection group, the Chattooga Conservancy, in 1994. "There were eight dams scheduled for the Chattooga," he tells me. "The river escaped those, but in other ways it is in worse shape now than when it was declared wild and scenic in 1974. The sediment loads just keep rising. We're in between the boomtowns of Atlanta and Greenville, and everyone looks to the mountains for second homes and recreation. We're getting more coliform bacteria and heavy metals from sewage as the towns build up."

Officials are finally beginning to look at the cumulative effects of both timber sales and rural developments upon the watershed. And both government agencies and private organizations have purchased land and easements along the WSR corridor. The Chattooga Conservancy's members are looking farther upstream, pushing to add more of the West Fork of the Chattooga to the existing WSR. They're also looking beyond the drainage to an array of other rivers that spill off the Southern Appalachians' Blue Ridge escarpment, some so full of waterfalls and cataracts that they make the Chattooga look tame. During the 1980s, conservationists succeeded in getting a short length of the Horsepasture designated as a WSR after a dam was proposed. Ultimately, they want to connect the Chattooga watershed by green corridors to Great Smoky Mountains National Park and the rest of the Blue Ridge highlands.

"You have to remember that this is one of the wildest areas left in the East," Williams says. "We've got to make people understand the importance of habitat linkages to animal movements and genetics, and we've got to do it in a hurry or we're pretty much going to run out of possibilities. Five years ago, if you said the words "land use management" or "zoning," you'd have had a riot on your hands. These are real independent folks around here. I mean, I've been caught in a Hatfields-and-McCoys-type cross fire between neighbors. But Atlanta's coming at all of us so fast, they're starting to listen."

YELLOWSTONE RIVER

One of the longest unfettered rivers in the lower 48 states, the Yellowstone flows 670 miles from the world's first national park to join the Missouri in North Dakota, meeting dams only in its final stretch. The upper reaches in Yellowstone National Park harbored almost every native animal except for one major predator, the wolf. Wolves were reintroduced during the mid-1990s, and they promptly made life harder for their smaller kin, the resident coyotes (below), whose numbers and territory size shrank as the wolves reclaimed their rightful niche.

*O*RLANDO IS COMING EVEN FASTER at Florida's Wekiva, designated a WSR in 2000. "Seminole County will be completely built out in about ten more years," says John Fillyaw, the manager of 42,000-acre Wekiva Basin Geo Park, which includes Wekiwa Springs State Park, Rock Springs Run State Reserve, and Lower Wekiva River Preserve State Park. "It makes what we can protect now all the more important." The process began in 1969, when the state purchased 6,400 acres around the crystalline Wekiwa Springs. Florida kept purchasing chunks of neighboring land over the years, just as acreage was added to a piece of property donated to the county around nearby Rock Springs, now a popular county park.

In 1988, the state passed the Wekiva River Protection Act, building upon that nucleus of reserves. Florida continued to add parcels here and there. The Audubon Society contributed a buffer area, and the St. Johns River Water Management District was acquiring land to ensure that enough of the natural water catchment area would remain intact to recharge flows and prevent them from drying up.

Fillyaw takes me on a brief tour to show off some of the vegetation communities preserved as a corollary of river basin conservation. They include sandhills, hardwood hammocks, longleaf pine and wire grass, and scrub oak. The countryside averages a little over 40 feet above sea level, and real estate developers home in on these slightly raised habitats like ants to a mound of sugar. Some have become so rare that a large percentage of their animal residents, from gopher tortoises and indigo snakes to snails, are listed as threatened or endangered. Fillyaw tells me, "We're trying to establish a wildlife corridor from here and the Seminole State Forest north to the 450,000-acre Ocala National Forest. It will be one of the biggest in the state, but that's the size we need if we're going to keep animals like the Florida black bear and river otter over the long run."

Through its Florida Forever initiative, the state has one of the most ambitious land acquisition programs for wildlife habitats and recreational opportunities in the nation. The ultimate plan is to link existing natural areas throughout the length and breadth of Florida, and rivers and their riparian corridors are the living ropes that will tie the pieces together. Florida boasts only one other national WSR, a short segment of the Loxahatchee east of Lake Okeechobee. However, the state has its own river and protection guidelines to go with an outstanding set of wildlife management areas, aquatic preserves, and canoe trails. Besides, scores of free-flowing Florida rivers such as the Apalachicola, the Sopchoppy, and the South Fork and the North Fork of the Saint Lucie remain candidates for WSR status in the future.

GOVERNMENT AGENCIES have identified 85,000 river miles eligible for WSR status nationwide. Although that amounts to just two-and-a-half percent of the total river miles in the U.S., it doesn' look as though there will be any shortage of possibilities for the system. The national advocacy group called American Rivers was originally formed to strengthen and expand the WSRA. It continues to do so in every state, although the organization's focus has shifted toward taking better care of rivers in general.

It appears that the heyday of government-sponsored dam building and grandiose water diversion projects may be behind us. Moreover, the Clean Water Act really has led to cleaner freshwater in many places. Yet a 1997 analysis by the Environmental Protection Agency (EPA) describes almost 40 percent of American rivers, lakes, and estuaries as unfit for fishing or swimming.

The chief culprit, which degrades 1.3 million miles of our waterways, is non-point source pollution. This is the stuff you can't trace to a particular sewage pipe or factory outflow. Like sediments from eroding logging roads, it washes into rivers one rainstorm or snowmelt or slow seep at a time from all over the place. It comes from farm fields sprayed with pesticides, livestock operations, and highways and parking lots splattered with the fluids that inevitably leak from cars. More trickles from millions of driveways, lawns, and trash-filled ditches, and from all the drainpipes and septic systems carrying the thousands of household chemicals that all of us pour into them. "Everything a society does winds up in the creek" is, to coin another saying, too true to be good.

The very air we breathe can foul the water nowadays. Carrying sulfur from exhaust fumes and, especially, coal-fired power plants, it drops acid rain onto lakes and streams *(Continued on page 188)*

COLORADO RIVER

Although the Grand Canyon escaped 20th-century impoundment schemes, another magnificent chasm upstream did not. Glen Canyon now lies drowned beneath Lake Mead. The Glen Canyon Dam also affected the Grand Canyon by blocking the normal pattern of flow, then abruptly releasing bursts for power generation that scoured away the Colorado's sandy shores downstream. Across the nation, rivers and the wildlife that feed and nest along their banks face the same dam problem. Still, the millions of years of geologic history on display in the Grand Canyon's walls offer perspective: Artificial impoundments aren't expected to last longer than a few human generations before they silt up and their usefulness comes to an end.

COLORADO RIVER *If your boat doesn't flip over in the Colorado, you're likely to*

get wet anyway once someone decides that bailing buckets were just made for a water fight.

(Continued from page 183) hundreds of miles distant. Virginia's Paine Run, for instance, is sick from acidification despite being located right in Shenandoah National Park. Levels of mercury in raindrops falling on New England sometimes exceed EPA standards for surface water. A powerful neurotoxin, this heavy metal reaches the atmosphere in smoke from waste incinerators and, again, coal-fired power plants, which provide about half the nation's electricity.

Finally, a large number of rivers are losing their vitality because their drainages are simply being overwhelmed by sprawl. There is no mega-hydro project or nasty waste dumper to rally against here either. No bad guys, no boondoggles. No corporate shenanigans to expose. Just us Americans—275 million of the fastest-growing population in any developed country.

*I*N THE END, THEN, the work of protecting rivers leads us to the same environmental issues most everyone is facing. Ours is a republic in search of more raw materials and consumer goods, more power, and more living space but also more clean air and water, more outdoor recreation, and more open space. In sum, we are a nation pressing up against the limits to growth, and what we need more of, above all else, are solutions.

Whatever the future brings, river conservation will be a major part of it. Whether you've ever been in a canoe or raft doesn't really matter. You're involved if you fish or bird-watch or swim or wade after frogs with your kids or just dangle an occasional toe in a passing stream. You never have? Okay, ignore the doggone fish. Forget all that yammering about ecosystems and biodiversity. As long as you drink water, you have a stake in the fate of our waterways. If only for our own sake, it would seem that we are obliged to leave as many as possible in at least as good shape as we found them.

Should we concentrate on setting aside additional wild and scenic rivers while the opportunity still exists? Or should the focus be on improving the long-term prospects of rivers that have already been designated by paying more attention to the rest of their watersheds? What about simply turning all our skills toward improving water quality in general? The answer people are choosing seems to be: all of the above.

*T*HE WSRA CONTINUES TO PLAY an invaluable role. And despite having been around for more than three decades, the system continues to set standards for innovation. In 1998 it added 81 miles of the Lumber River in North Carolina. The primary responsibility for management falls upon that state, which began the protection process back in 1978, declaring the popular canoeing destination its first recreational water trail. Three years later, the Lumber became a National Water Trail, and in 1989 it joined the state's system of special waterways under the North Carolina Natural and Scenic Rivers Act, modeled after the federal program.

The Lumber is the essence of a swampy black-water realm—a slow, tannin-stained flow through a bottomland hardwood forest where Spanish moss drapes from the branches of cypress trees. Gators stir the bottom beside rare mussels and two uncommon fish, the pinewoods darter and sandhills chub. Endangered red-cockaded woodpeckers drill nesting cavities in the old pines of the higher spots. As the first WSR on the Atlantic coastal plain between New Jersey and Florida, it symbolizes the trend toward broadening the national system to make it more representative of the country's different bio-regions.

The year 1999 saw the addition of Massachusetts' Sudbury, Assabet, and Concord WSR complex, an example of community-based action to reinvigorate a hard-used waterway in a long-developed countryside. In 2000 much the same sort of effort culminated in the designation of 191 miles of White Clay Creek and its tributaries, running through farmlands and small towns in southeastern Pennsylvania and northeastern Delaware. The waterway, its corridor, and its 21 species of native fish accommodate hikers, birders, picnickers, and skiers while still providing residents with reliable drinking water. Along with Florida's Wekiva, 23.3 miles of the mountain stream called Wilson Creek, in North Carolina, joined the system in 2000 as well. So did 13.9 miles of Wildhorse and Kiger Creeks on Bureau of Land Management range country in Oregon.

The next addition may be the Taunton River, which drains a 562-square-mile watershed with 38 different towns and cities in Massachusetts. It is another Atlantic coast waterway, emptying into

"The care of rivers is not a question of rivers, but of the human heart."
—Tanaka Shozo.
Drifting close to sleep, a pair of low-tech river explorers share the glow of northeastern Michigan's Platte River.

Mount Hope Bay in Rhode Island. Perhaps surprisingly, given its proximity to such a dense human population, it is also another source of clear drinking water, one that becomes all the more valuable with each passing year. Congress just passed legislation authorizing a formal WSR study, the usual prelude to official designation.

Reflecting a clear trend in the national system, the Taunton's supporters want community-based groups rather than government agencies to direct management of the river. This looks like the Sudbury, Assabet, and Concord all over again—a grassroots effort to figure out how to maintain natural values in the midst of rapid growth. A proposal for a WSR study of Eightmile River, a tributary of the Connecticut River, is working its way through Congress at the moment, and it, too, began with townsfolk anxious to counter the effects of sprawl.

E ARLIER STAGES OF RIVER PROTECTION can be found across the country. No one can say up until the final negotiations are over how successful they will prove to be. Anything is possible. I never thought that in my lifetime society would start breaching dams to restore the flow of rivers and the future of migratory fish. Along with hundreds of minor impoundments and some obsolete dams, one of the most significant barriers to come down was the Edwards Dam on Maine's Kennebec River. A dam on the Elwha River of Washington's Olympic Peninsula, where 100-pound chinook salmon used to spawn, may be torn down within the next few years, and fisheries experts have suggested removing four dams on the Snake River as part of the effort to save the last salmon runs on that branch of the Columbia River system.

None of us knows the perfect way to treat rivers in order to balance our multitude of desires. The amazing, magnificent, supremely optimistic thing is that people are trying. Granted, they could probably work smarter and argue less. Possibly, they could learn to accommodate even more economic demands and still keep rivers beautiful and free-flowing and animated by miraculous creatures of all kinds. Until then, though, they are doing the best they know how, and we have wild and scenic waters to carry us through the years ahead.

ALTAMAHA RIVER Easing toward the Atlantic south of Savannah, Georgia, under a

peach-colored horizon, the Altamaha seems to become one with the soft and sultry coastal plain.

YELLOWSTONE RIVER *Like trumpeter swans, America's rivers are recovering from a 20th-century low point*

through protective measures designed to ensure that their strength, grace, and purity will always be part of our lives.

NOTES ON THE CONTRIBUTORS

Douglas H. Chadwick has a home by the shore of a wild and scenic Montana river and reared two children in a cabin there with his wife, Karen Reeves. It was when he traveled to Washington, D.C., as a private citizen during the 1970s to testify for river protection at a Senate hearing that Chadwick won his first assignment for NATIONAL GEOGRAPHIC magazine. A wildlife biologist, he has since written nearly 40 articles on animals, ecosystems, and conservation for the magazine. He is also the author of several National Geographic books, most recently *Yellowstone to Yukon.*

In the past three years, **Raymond Gehman** has photographed nine rivers for National Geographic books. Gehman began his career at the Society as an intern in 1979 and scored a NATIONAL GEOGRAPHIC magazine assignment that same year. His first book assignment was in 1984. When he's not on a river, he lives with his wife and two sons in Waynesboro, Pennsylvania.

Brian Peterson is a staff photographer at the Minneapolis *Star-Tribune.* Eight times named Minnesota Press Photographer of the Year and recipient of the 1996 Canon Photo Essay award and the 1995 Robert F. Kennedy Journalism award in photojournalism, he lives in Minneapolis with his wife and three daughters. This is his first assignment for National Geographic.

ACKNOWLEDGMENTS

The author would like to thank, first and foremost, Kristen McDonald of American Rivers for information, advice, and a careful reading of the manuscript for accuracy. Gratitude is also due Ian Kean of the River League for a continuing flow of news about northern rivers and conservation issues in general. River trips bind together those who share the daily challenges and camp routines, and photographer Ray Gehman helped make the two voyages we covered jointly as journalists especially memorable. I wish to thank my wife, Karen Reeves, for many good years of co-paddling many good rivers, and my daughter, Teal I. Chadwick, for assisting me in travel to—and down—a variety of waterways for this book. Whatever understanding I gained of rivers and of the wild lives and human freedoms they sustain across our nation is largely due to the array of people mentioned in the text. Of those, let me also state here that two longtime friends of the National Geographic Society, John C. Craighead and Frank C. Craighead, are in many respects the fathers of our National Wild and Scenic Rivers System and, as such, have greatly benefited all Americans. John's son, John W. Craighead, was of particular help to me as I conducted my research.

ILLUSTRATION CREDITS

Cover, R.G.K. Photography/stone; 1, Brian Peterson; 2-3, Jim Richardson; 4-5, Phil Schermeister. Chapter One: 6-7, Chris Anderson/AURORA; 8, Phil Schermeister; 9, Brian Peterson; 14-19 (all), Raymond Gehman; 22, David Muench; 23, Peter Essick/AURORA; 27, Phil Schermeister; 28-29, Robert Mackinlay/Peter Arnold, Inc.; 32-33, David Muench; 34-35, Raymond Gehman; 35, Yvette Cardozo/stone; 36-37, Joel Sartore/www.joelsartore.com; 40-41, William Albert Allard, National Geographic Photographer; 45-47 (all), Brian Peterson; 50-51, David Muench; 54-55 & 55, Phil Schermeister; 56, Peter Essick/AURORA; 56-57, Bob Krist; 58-61 (all), Raymond Gehman. Chapter Two: All photographs by Raymond Gehman. Chapter Three: All photographs by Raymond Gehman. Chapter Four: All photographs by Brian Peterson. Chapter Five: 154-155, Daniel J. Cox/stone; 156, Bert Sagara/stone; 157-165 (all), Raymond Gehman; 168-169, Jim Richardson; 170-171, Charles Gurche; 172-173 (all), Joel Sartore/www.joelsartore.com; 176-177, Bruce Dale/NGS Image Collection; 177, David Epperson/stone; 180 & 181, Annie Griffiths Belt; 184-185, Bruce Dale; 186-187, Melissa Farlow; 191, Mark R. Godfrey; 192-193, Peter Essick; 194-195, Annie Griffiths Belt; 196, Raymond Gehman.

In a warm spring by the edge of the Rio Grande in Texas, the author soaks away miles and days of hard paddling, river mud, and Chihuahuan Desert dust. "I doubt this picture would convince anybody," he says, "but I really do work for a living."

Index

Boldface indicates illustrations.

Exploring America's
Wild & Scenic Rivers

By Douglas H. Chadwick

Published by the National Geographic Society
John M. Fahey, Jr. *President and Chief Executive Officer*
Gilbert M. Grosvenor *Chairman of the Board*
Nina D. Hoffman *Executive Vice President*

Prepared by the Book Division
Kevin Mulroy *Vice President and Editor-in-Chief*
Charles Kogod *Illustrations Director*
Barbara A. Payne *Editorial Director*
Marianne R. Koszorus *Design Director*

Staff for this Book
Rebecca Lescaze *Editor*
Sadie Quarrier *Illustrations Editor*
Suez Kehl Corrado *Art Director*
Victoria Garrett Jones *Researcher*
Carl Mehler *Director of Maps*
Matt Chwastyk, Thomas L. Gray, Tibor G. Tóth,
Gregory Ugiansky, Martin S. Walz
Map Research and Production
R. Gary Colbert *Production Director*
Richard S. Wain *Production Project Manager*
Cynthia M. Combs, Meredith C. Wilcox
Illustrations Coordinators
Julia Marshall *Indexer*

Manufacturing and Quality Control
George V. White *Director*
Alan V. Kerr, Vincent P. Ryan *Managers*
Phillip L. Schlosser *Financial Analyst*

Library of Congress Cataloging-in-Publication Data
Chadwick, Douglas H.
    Exploring America's wild and scenic rivers / by Douglas H. Chadwick.
        p. cm.
    Includes bibliographical references (p.).
    ISBN 0-7922-7880-1 (reg.) -- ISBN 0-7922-7881-X (dlx.)
    1. Wild and scenic rivers—United States. 2. Untied States—Description and travel. I.
    Title: Exploring America's wild and scenic rivers. II. Title: Wild and scenic rivers. III. Title.

    QH76 .C38 2001
    333.78'45'0973—dc21   2001044091

The world's largest nonprofit scientific and educational organization, the National Geographic Society was founded in 1888 "for the increase and diffusion of geographic knowledge." Since then it has supported scientific exploration and spread information to its more than eight million members worldwide.

The National Geographic Society educates and inspires millions every day through magazines, books, television programs, videos, maps and atlases, research grants, the National Geographic Bee, teacher workshops, and innovative classroom materials.

The Society is supported through membership dues, charitable gifts, and income from the sale of its educational products.

Members receive NATIONAL GEOGRAPHIC magazine—the Society's official journal—discounts on Society products, and other benefits.

For more information about the National Geographic Society, its educational programs, publications, or ways to support its work, please call 1-800-NGS-LINE (647-5463), or write to the following address:

National Geographic Society
1145 17th Street N.W.
Washington, D.C. 20036-4688
U.S.A.

Visit the Society's Web site at
www.nationalgeographic.com

Composition for this book by the National Geographic Society Book Division. Printed and bound by R.R. Donnelley & Sons, Willard, Ohio. Color separations by Quad Graphics, Martinsburg, West Virginia. Dust jacket printed by Miken Companies, Inc., Cheektowaga, New York.